I Remember

CANTRICE N. COSTIN

Published by:
Cantrice N. Costin
cantricecostin1974@gmail.com

ISBN:

DEDICATIONS PAGE

First off, I would like to give all glory to God for keeping me focused and driven throughout this process. This book is dedicated to Him for always keeping me sane, even in my worst moments. This is also dedicated to all 11 of my children, who make me proud more and more each day. To my parents, thank you for raising me to be the woman I am today and someone who my children can look up to. Lastly, I dedicate this book to myself. The old me would be so proud of who I've become. I've survived all the hurdles that life has thrown at me and gracefully overcome adversity. So, to God, my children, Eboni, Natasha, Amber, Theresa, Javon, Dashawn, Tamar, Jada, Jayden, Teonna, Aniyah, and my parents, Darlene and Otis, this one is for you.

Chapter 1

So where do I start? I guess I will start from the beginning, from where my memories began. I remember the family barbecues. I remember playing in the woods with my cousins. I remember going to church with my grandma. I remember the endless doctor visits and hospital stays. I remember mommy and daddy arguing all the time. I remember so many things. But, what I remember the most is the love that I always felt as a child. The sweet smell of the honeysuckles, the beautiful sunflowers, the smell of the water from the neighborhood baby pool; all the beautiful and exotic animals from the local zoo always amazed me every time my dad would take us there. I remember when my cousins and I used to get in trouble for not listening. Grandma would make us go in the woods and get a switch and beat us with it. I would usually be the one to get out of getting a beating because I would use my asthma to my advantage. "Grandma, I'm wheezing! Grandma, I can't breathe!" Yeah, having asthma got me out of a lot of things.

I loved my cousins so much on both sides of my family—my mom and my dad's side. Both sides were more than just cousins to me. They were like my other siblings. We always had a good time whenever we were together. I mean, of course, we had our little arguments and fistfights but we always made up about an hour later. We could not stay mad at one another for too long. Everyone always felt sorry for me because I could not always go out and play, and if I could go out, I could never play for too long. This asthma was a curse to me.

I was always a sickly child suffering from asthma. I missed out on a lot. But mommy and daddy always made me feel special. I remember mommy always telling me stories and daddy trying to sing but always ended up whistling every song to me. They were always there and I never once heard them complain. When I used to get so sad watching the other kids play from my window, my mommy knew. She would always come to me and say, "Gilly, are you hungry? You want to watch the stories with me? Daddy knew as well. He would say, "Come here. Let me show you a trick with these here cards." I loved, and still love them from my soul.

Yeah, having asthma made me feel so lonely. I remember missing so many days of school. I remember seeing this illness as a big bubble and thinking one day I was going to cough it up and the asthma would be gone! Oh, but I was so wrong! That would not be the case up to this very day. I knew my eldest sister resented me for taking up so much of mommy and daddy's attention all the time. But little did she know this was not the attention that I was seeking.

I came from what I felt like were two of the biggest families in our little town of Bridgeton, New Jersey. The Costins and the Germans. I have two sisters, Tanisha and Keyonna. I'm the middle child. My mother's name is Darlene Marie Costin and my daddy's name is Lee Otis German. I loved both sides of the family for so many different reasons. Comparing the two was like night and day. Costins are calm, somewhat quiet, and reserved. I would say it took a lot to get them upset and to the point of becoming violent.

The Germans are rowdy, argumentative, and fighters. You could look at them the wrong way and that was all it took; you had a fight on your hands. I inherited traits from both sides. Now about my sisters. My eldest sister is a fighter, the mean one. We fought a lot. She always won. I know now she was only trying to make me tough. I remember her hitting me up side my head with a lamp one time. I also remember when she tried to set me on fire. I can remember all the fights we had. She would always scratch my face up. I believe she did that because I was always the prettier sister. But, what I remember most as far as my sister is concerned is that she always had my back. She was my bodyguard. My protector. My hero. Even with my asthma, I was always in some kind of altercation. It was like I had to prove to myself and everyone else that just because I had asthma did not mean I could not be tough. I remember when I would get short of breath from fighting, my sister was always there to take over and finish what I always started—always coming to my rescue.

Now, my little sister is the one I felt I had to protect at all costs no matter what. My Boop, the baby girl. She was the quiet one, standoffish, kept to herself. Still that way to this very day. But sweet and kind. Boop was everyone's baby. Especially mommy and daddy. We loved her so much because she was the baby. Me, I guess I would be a little of both of them; quiet, mean, standoffish, and a fighter. We knew we could not go home and tell daddy we had a fight and we lost. That was unacceptable in daddy's eyes. We had to always win. If we did not win we knew what was in store for us. No way did we want to face daddy's wrath. So, we never lost a fight.

We moved around a lot but within the same town. My siblings and I spent a lot of time with both sides of the family. I have so many fond memories.

One of my fondest memories was one hot summer day when mommy was at work and I had a horrible asthma attack. We had no car, and no phone. There was no 9-1-1 back in those days, which were in the late 70s. I remember my dad putting me on his shoulders and walking me to the emergency room. All I could think of at that moment was, my daddy is so strong; my daddy is my hero, and my daddy must love me because he never took a break. He just kept walking until we got to the front door of the hospital.

Another fond memory I have is of me and my sister staying up late waiting for my mom to get off work; waiting because we missed her but also because we knew she would have those huge windmill cookies in the shape of a baseball player swinging a bat. My sister and I loved those cookies. Mommy would always have the cookies wrapped up in aluminum foil. She would come into our room and sit on the edge of the bed and ask us what we did that day. After giving us our cookies she would say three things: goodnight, say your prayers, and I love you. My sweet dear mama.

The memories were not always good. I vividly remember one night when I was 3-years old. Mommy was at work and daddy was playing his music and drinking with his best friend. My sister and I were in the room playing. Daddy ran out of his beer so he went to the store to get more and asked his best friend to watch us. I remember him calling my name so I went to see what he wanted. I felt comfortable around him. After all, that was my daddy's friend.

He was around every day. I remember him asking me to come sit on his lap so I did. He pulled out his penis and told me to touch it. At that exact moment my sister walked in and witnessed what was happening. He nervously placed his penis back in his pants. My sister yelled for me to come to her. When daddy got back my sister told my dad what had happened. I remember my uncles and my aunt coming over. I remember arguing going back and forth. I felt this was all my fault. I don't know to this very day what they did to that man, but what I do know is that he never came around after that night.

Another memory I have is when our home caught on fire. We lost everything. Our neighbor who lived above us fell asleep while popping popcorn. We got out with only the clothes we had on our backs. I remember our next-door neighbor being kind enough to give us blankets as we all stood watching our home burn down to the ground. My mom's sister showed up along with another family member. They argued about who we were going to stay with. I remember standing there just watching and listening to them argue. How could they be arguing at a time like this when we were homeless and penniless? Suddenly I remember my dad's mom, my other grandma, pulled up in her long car. She took me and my sister by the hands and placed us in her car. She did not say anything to anyone. My grandma Unell was a godsend that night. I remember her buying us new clothes and taking care of us for a while until my mom got back on her feet. But for those few weeks I do not know where Mommy was. I just remember her coming over every day and visiting with us.

Mommy finally found a new home and she came and got us. Not soon after that my baby sister was born. We were so happy. The year was 1979. The house we were living in was huge but also haunted, but that's another story. I started spending a lot of time at home with mommy because my asthma had gotten worse. I know it was my mommy's prayers that saved my life every time I ended up in the hospital, along with God's mercy and His grace. I'm not exactly sure how long we lived in that house but I do remember being so happy when we moved. We did have good times in that house though. I remember the huge barn that was in the backyard. We were told daily to stay out of the barn because it wasn't safe, but we never listened. We played hide n' seek in that barn on many days. The house was so big to us that we even played hide n' seek in the house, too. Yeah, those were the good old days.

Mommy always made sure we went to church no matter where we lived and no matter what was going on. Mommy always read her Bible and prayed. I remember her always sleeping with the Bible under her pillow. Mommy instilled in us the Word of God and His power at an early age. Mommy taught us the power of prayer. We grew up in a Baptist church, going to church at least three days a week. We loved going to church. I remember the Saturday nights of getting our hair washed and straightened with that hot comb. That horrible smell of our hair burning and our ears getting burned by that hot comb, and Mommy and Grandma always saying, "Hush, it's only the Blue Magic hair grease." Mommy always dressed me and my oldest sister alike for every holiday. We hated it. But we loved putting on those brand-new clothes.

The move to Camden, New Jersey is when I started to notice the distance between mommy and daddy. The arguments got more intense. In fact, the arguments got so bad at one point I remember mommy busting daddy upside his head with a huge, glass crystal vase. I remember me and my sister picking the glass out of his head, and I was crying at the same time, thinking to myself, why would mommy hurt my daddy like this? I found out years later that Daddy had a white girlfriend on the side, and he had been taking food out of our home to feed her and her family.

One of my younger aunts moved in with us because she became pregnant at a young age. Mommy took care of her and her baby. We ended up moving back to Bridgeton. Mommy and Daddy broke up soon after that. I guess Mommy grew tired of his drinking and cheating. I remember Daddy having a few different girlfriends. But he made sure they treated us well. We were daddy's girls. Daddy made sure he would always pick us up on our birthdays and take us to Big John's Pizza. I can only remember mommy dating one man at that time. Mommy worked a lot and she did not have time to date.

I remember this one particular winter that was brutally cold and we had a few snowstorms. Mommy took on a second job to make ends meet and to make sure we had a decent Christmas. I did not know what that second job was until one night I went into the bathroom and saw her trying to take off her socks and shoes. Mommy could not do it because her hands were too cold. So I did it for her. I found out later that she would stand in the cold for hours ringing a Salvation Army bell to make money for us. I remember my heartbreak for her when I found out. Mommy always did her best to take care of us.

Mommy had such a kind heart. She took care of 10 out of 13 of her siblings at different times in her life. Mommy even took in their children, her nieces and nephews. She loved her family. To me, she was the only child out of 15 children who looked exactly like her father. There were times when Mommy took money that she had saved for rainy days because her siblings were in need and helped them out. She had to make sure her younger siblings, nieces and nephews had what they needed. Mommy was so selfless and kind. Her favorite line was, "I'll give a dog a bone." In my eyes my mom was perfect. I remember even when she worked all day she would show up at the hospital at night if I was there to see about me. And there were many of those nights. I never heard her complain ever. I would be so happy whenever she walked through that hospital door. It would feel like my heart would leap and the tears would well up in my eyes because my hero had arrived. I could finally relax and go to sleep.

I remember the cookouts and barbecues for every holiday. Mommy made sure we would always have brand new matching outfits. Grandpa would be on the grill and his food was always so delicious. We always had so much food. Everyone always had a good time. Love, laughter, and fun. I have never to this day tasted grilled food better than my grandpops food.

My grandpa is the father of 15 children. I remember the long hot, boring summer afternoons when Grandpa would lay on the couch watching his baseball games. Oh, how he loved baseball.

His favorite team was the Phillies. He would call me Gillsticks. Grandpa always wanted his hair scratched. I guess that's where I get it from. I had to be the one to do it. He would always say, "Come scratch your pop pop's hair." I felt special because out of all the grandkids he would always ask me. Grandpa had the most beautiful soft curly hair; that's where my mom got her beautiful long hair from.

I loved being at my grandparent's house as a child. Grandma always took me and my sister to church with her. I remember us always having to sing the same two songs over and over again in front of the church. We used to be so nervous walking up there and singing. I don't know why they would ask us to sing because we absolutely could not sing.

As we got older I noticed a change in my grandma. She would pick and choose who could stay the night at her house. My sister and I used to be told we couldn't stay a lot, that only certain grandkids could stay. It used to hurt my feelings so bad that I would cry. It made me feel like she didn't like us, or maybe she didn't even love us. But grandpa never made me feel that way. I remember him always bringing us those huge, sweet watermelons, long stalks of sugarcane, and crabs. I remember him bringing us a Christmas tree every year with oranges and apples. And I can't forget the pecans and walnuts he used to bring for us.

My grandma Unell, my dad's mom, she always made us feel special and welcome. She did not have favorites; she loved us all equally. And you talk about cooking, my grandma would throw down in that kitchen. I remember her always cooking so much food. If you asked for food, you had to eat everything she put on that plate or you would sit at the table until you ate it all—or either feel her wrath with the switches. Everything she made was delicious. I don't care if it was a peanut butter and jelly sandwich. It was delicious because it was done out of love.

Between my mom and my dad's family, I have 13 aunts and 8 uncles. I believe the aunts on my mom's side loved us back then, but they surely don't now. I will explain why I believe that a little later on in my story. I also believe the 5 aunts on my daddy's side loved us then, but except for one, I'm not so sure about now. I know without a doubt that one aunt she loved us then and now.

As far as my uncles on my mama's side, I don't know if they ever loved us, then or now. But, the uncles on my daddy's side always loved us.

I remember when one of my aunts on my mom's side got married because she got pregnant at a young age. That morning was epic. One of my uncles ended up beating her soon-to-be husband on the morning of the wedding, right on my grandparent's front lawn. I was too young to know the reason why they were fighting.

There were many fights that I witnessed as a child on both sides of my family. I also remember my sister fighting one of my uncles' daughter on my mom's side of the family. My sister beat her up pretty bad. As you can imagine, that did not sit well with my uncle. Mommy was at work and I'm not sure where daddy was at the time, because had he been home, this surely would not have happened. We were home with our babysitter. After the fight my uncle came to our house. We lived right next door to one another. He beat my sister so badly with an electric cord. Daddy finally made it back home and when he came into the house, he saw the welts all over my sister's body. Daddy became enraged. Daddy went next door and dragged my uncle out of the house and beat him so badly in the middle of the street. I remember after they finally stopped fighting daddy threw him in a trashcan. Once again I saw my dad as my hero. After God, my daddy was my first love and my first hero. Despite all his drinking, I loved him with everything in me.

My daddy was a dog lover. I remember we had several dogs growing up. We had two rottweilers that we named Starsky and Hutch after our favorite TV show at the time. We had a chow we named Snowball. He looked like a furry white ball. We would later give him to my grandma because his fur was causing me to have major asthma attacks. She would later rename him Fluffy. Daddy would also bring this huge Great Dane to the house named Tempest. Tempest was not ours but you couldn't tell us that because daddy would always have her. But the dog that my daddy loved the most was our little chihuahua named Killer. And that he was; the name fit him perfectly. Killer made sure no one got too close to us. He was especially protective of daddy. Daddy loved that dog. Our next-door neighbor would end up poisoning our dog. At least that's the story we were told because she said Killer had bitten her son when he and daddy were shadow boxing. That would be the first time I saw daddy cry. It was heartbreaking to see him sitting on the edge of the tub trying to hide his tears and pain. That would also be our last dog as children.

Life would go on. My hospital stays became more frequent, and the cookouts and family barbeques never ceased. Spending quality time with my family continued. But I loved life despite asthma and many hospital stays. Mommy continued to work hard and daddy continued to drink. It was like I didn't have a care in the world until Mommy started dating this one particular person that I didn't care for. He was weird.

I noticed that when he started to come around odd things would happen. Eerie cold unexplained drafts in the house. I would hear unexplained noises coming from the basement. We would see dark shadows and we would start to call "The Shadows". It was so scary. He asked mommy to marry him. Thank God she didn't. He ended up passing away. But nothing would be scarier than mommy choosing to move us away from New Jersey to Connecticut, away from our family, and mainly away from my daddy.

Chapter 2

So, here we are in Connecticut. The year is 1985. And I'm like, wow, I can't believe I'm away from my daddy. It hurt and I was so angry with mommy. I wondered if I would ever see my daddy again. I remember thinking, this cannot be real. Mommy moved us to a place that was foreign to us. I cried so hard. I just wanted to be back with my daddy and the rest of my family. But one good thing about our move was that my aunt and her three kids, my cousins, came to Connecticut. with us. We moved into a building that one of my mom's other sisters owned and had agreed to rent to my mom and my aunt. It was there that I would meet my first love.

So life went on. Mommy found a job. The economy was booming in Connecticut back in the 80s. Jobs were available everywhere and the pay was great too, which was the main reason my mom and auntie moved to Connecticut. I remember mommy cooking on the weekends for several different clubs to make extra money. Everyone loved my mom's special potato salad. They would say no one could make it like Muff. Muff was my mommy's nickname.

Mommy loved going out to those clubs. We started making friends and things started to look up. That is until that dreadful night that Mommy brought "him" home. I remember the very first time I laid eyes on "him." I instantly got goosebumps all over my body. I started having heart palpitations, sweating, and I felt a fear come over me that I had never felt before. This fear would eventually grow into hatred for "him." Mommy continued to date "him" and as their relationship got more serious, he started to come around more often. I remember one time when they broke up for a short period and mommy started seeing someone else. This particular night he must have been following mommy and her new friend. Mommy was sitting outside in the car with her new friend and he snuck up behind the car with a cloth bag filled with rocks. He then proceeded to throw the rocks at the car windows. He and mommy's friend started to violently fight. We all watched from the windows. The neighbors also watched in amusement. I remember being horrified by what I was witnessing. That incident further let me know this man was crazy, possessive, and dangerous. But mommy got back with "him."

When we moved to our new home, to my horror, he moved in with us. That decision that mommy made would lead to many years of nothing but trouble. It started with him not wanting us to touch his food and if we did it would lead to arguments. At this point, I was 10-years-old and my sisters were 11 and 5. I remember mommy getting an overnight job making car parts and we were left home with him at night. We began to notice him watching us as we walked around the house. We noticed he did that at night when he thought we were asleep. We noticed him trying to get into our room but we always remembered to lock the door when mommy left for work because we didn't trust him. I remember him always twisting and turning the doorknobs. We began to sleep in shifts. Me and my eldest sister would take turns sleeping and watch the door to make sure Keyonna was safe. I remember us pushing our dresser in front of the door to keep him out. I hated him. I remember having dreams of him disappearing. I wanted him out of our lives. I lived in fear every day. I was not concerned about me or my older sister. My main concern was my baby sister. I needed to protect her. I had to protect her. I was so unhappy.

We moved again. It is there that he would put a gun to my head and attempt to rape me. I remember that night like it was yesterday. Mommy was at work and he asked me to go into the basement to get an extension cord for the Christmas tree. So, being obedient, I went down to the basement to get the cord. But on my way back up the basement steps, he was coming down the steps toward me. I did not notice the gun at first until he got closer to me. Then I saw it and I felt pure, deep terror. He put the gun to my left temple and told me to kiss him. I started to tremble. Then all of a sudden my Savior God Himself had a "ram in the bush for me." My neighbor who lived on the first floor opened the basement door and I saw her and my baby sister standing there. I know that was no one but GOD! This lady never came out of her house; she needed assistance to walk. In the two years we had lived there, I only had seen her twice. When he saw her and my sister he ran out the side door of the basement. I ran up the steps, grabbed my sister, and pushed her up the stairs. I told her to go to her room. I went to call my mom at her job and tell her what had just happened. I remember the words Mommy said; she said that she would handle it. I then went into mom's room and went to a shoebox at the top of her closet. I removed a gun from there and to this day I don't even remember how I knew that the gun was there. I sat on the bed and put the gun to my head. I was going to shoot myself. I was not even afraid. It's like I was moving in slow motion. Then I heard a voice say to me, *"What about Keyonna?"* Then I thought of my baby sister. I thought, who is going to protect her from him? I placed the gun back in the shoebox, thinking mommy is coming home and she's going to make him pay for what he did. But, I was so wrong. He came back through the door that same night smiling and walking behind mommy. His smile was so sinister. Mommy looked straight ahead and went into her room. She did not look at me or ask me any questions. We never addressed the issue again. What took place was never spoken of, ever. I remember crying so hard. I felt so alone. I wanted my daddy. I wanted my daddy to come and rescue us but that never happened.

Not long after that horrible thing happened to me, one cold night there was a blizzard that winter. He got angry with my baby sister about something; my aunt and cousins were living with us at the time. He started to beat on her with the famous extension cord. I got so angry! My sisters and my cousin and I jumped on him. He got away from us somehow and went into the room to get his gun. I remember Mommy yelling for us to run. We ran out of the house without a coat in a blizzard without my baby sister. He had actually pulled a gun out on four children, which would not be the last time. We stayed at my friend's house for three days until the police came knocking on her door looking for us. My mom had told them we ran away but she left out the fact that he was abusing us, trying to molest and rape us, and neglected to tell the authorities that he pulled his gun out on us. At the time that these things were happening to us, all I could think of was my daddy. Why was daddy not coming to get us? Why wasn't daddy here to hurt this man? I wanted this man to go away by any means necessary. I wanted him dead.

Not long after that I started dating Jack. I had already known him. I lost my virginity to him. Jack became my hero, my protector, my provider, my king, my everything. Jack made me feel safe. He gave me whatever I wanted. He was a few years older than me but that didn't matter to me. I wanted to be with him all day, every day.

In the beginning, I never told Jack what I was going through at home because I thought he would not want to be with me anymore. We stayed at a hotel a lot, or he would sneak me into his house to his bedroom. I would ask the lady across the street from us if she could watch my baby sister. I did not want either of us to be left alone in the house with "him." My older sister was always gone. She was barely around and my mom said she was out of control, so she ended up sending my sister back to New Jersey to live with my aunt. I truly believe that "he" talked my mom into sending her away so he could do things to me and my baby sister. You see, he would not touch my older sister.. She was the fighter. But, I always wondered why she really sent her away. Mommy told me it was because she never wanted to listen, and was always in the streets, but so was I. Why didn't I get sent away with her? I don't know if I will ever have the answer to that question.

I remember the only time my mom allowed my best friend to stay the night and "he" was caught peeking through the heater vent while she bathed. My friend was horrified and she was never allowed to stay the night again. Soon after that one of my aunts came down from New Jersey with her two sons. My aunt needed a place to stay. I remember mommy saying "yes" as she always did. I never understood why they all had to stay with us and never with other siblings. As I recall, they only came with a small duffel bag of clothes and no heavy coats in the middle of winter. It was close to Christmas so mommy took some of the money she had saved for our Christmas gifts and bought my cousins what she could. I didn't have a problem with it. I just looked at mommy and said, "Oh how I love this woman." Her heart was kind and giving.

One morning about 3 or 4 am, I began to hear my aunt screaming my mom's name. She screamed so loudly she woke us up out of our sleep. "He" had struck again. He tried to rape my auntie this time. I remember mommy kicking my aunt out of the house. Mommy acted as if she did not believe my aunt. But, I believed her. I knew she was not lying. Again, nothing was done to him. I began to wonder what type of hold he had on her. I would find out years later. Eventually, my aunt moved back into our home.

It was now 1986. I was hanging out and staying out. Not coming home because I didn't want to be in the same space as "him." My aunt was there so I could relax as far as my baby sister was concerned because my aunt would keep a watchful eye out for her. We kind of got to know his cousin's children as we were all in the same age group.

One particular incident I can recall is when his cousins got into a fight with some other neighborhood kids and he felt that we should help them fight. We said no and he became so angry that he stomped off into the room. Something in me said, Run! I grabbed my baby sister's hand and my eldest sister was right behind us. We ran and we ran fast because I knew he was going for his gun. He was always going for that gun. The gun was his protector; it was also his way of trying to scare us and control us. We were running in the rain. It was dark and stormy. I remember seeing the lightning flashing across the night sky as we hid behind bushes. He was following us in his car. It was like we were his prey and he was the hunter. We made it safely to my aunt's house who lived about 15 minutes away. We banged on her door, soaking wet. We explained to her what had happened. She immediately called my mother in a rage. I remember my mom getting off work and coming to my aunt's house. My mom and my aunt argued. We went back home and again, nothing was said or done to him. I began to wonder if anyone cared about our safety. Were we not important? I began to question if my mama loved us anymore. She always protected him but what about us, her children?

It is now 1987. This is the year I became pregnant at the age of 13. I was scared. I was not scared of becoming a mom. I was scared of my mom's anger as she hated and despised Jack. I finally got up the nerve to tell Mommy. The words that she would say to me would haunt me for years to come. My mama said that I had to go get an abortion. She called the police on Jack and accused him of statutory rape. "He" was even angrier than Mommy because in his eyes, I was no longer pure and he couldn't take from me what he had always wanted, which were my innocence and virginity. Mommy made me an appointment to get an abortion, and gave me bus fare to get there, but she didn't come with me. Jack came with me. That bus ride seemed so long. I was scared and disappointed. Jack looked at me and saw the fear and hurt in my eyes. He then pulled that skinny wire on the bus which alerts the driver that you're at your destination and needed to get off. We got off the bus and he said, "You are not doing this. We are not killing our baby." I was so happy and yet so afraid. I was afraid to go back home with this baby growing inside of me.

I remember walking in the door. I dared not bring Jack with me. Mommy may have tried to kill him. I broke the news to mommy and she looked at me with what looked to be disgust and hatred. Her words to me were, "I'm not gonna help you with that baby. That baby will be born ugly, black, and with a big nose." My mom was disappointed in me. I knew it. I could see it in her eyes. It hurt me so bad that she couldn't or wouldn't look at me. Mommy would never look at me the same again.

I became excited about the baby. I began reading baby books. Jack and his sisters began buying baby clothes. Mommy never came with me to any of my prenatal appointments. I wanted mommy to be happy for me about the baby, but she was not happy at all. The pregnancy was going well with no serious complications. I noticed "him" watching me with disgust as my stomach grew bigger and bigger. I recall one time we got into an argument, I don't remember why. But I remember him knocking me to the floor and pouncing on me. I was eight months pregnant, and he proceeded to choke me. My mom and my aunt had to pull him off of me. All I could do was cry. I ran to the phone to call Jack. Jack got to my house in less than 10 minutes with his father and brother. My mom would not allow me to go downstairs to him, so they came upstairs, but mommy would not open the door. I believe they would have killed him had they gotten in the house. My mom was so upset with me for calling Jack that she called the police on them. Jack went to jail that day. What I could not understand was how she could call the police on them for trying to protect me, but not call the police on him for trying to strangle me to death. Again, I could not understand the hold he had on her.

When it came close to the time for the baby to be born, Mommy decided to take a trip down south to North Carolina with "him." While Mommy was in North Carolina, I went into labor. What a coincidence. The childbirth was so painful. I was scared because mommy was not there. Who would hold me and tell me I was going to be okay? Jack finally arrived and so did my auntie. I would forever be grateful to her for standing in in place of my mommy. She and Jack were there to support me. I was so grateful, but I still needed and wanted my mommy.

I would have my baby on "his" birthday. The only person I hated in this whole wide world and my baby had to be born on his birthday. I gave birth to a beautiful 5 pound 12-ounce baby girl. My baby was the complete opposite of what Mommy had spoken over her. I named her Eboni. She was a high yellow, light-skinned baby with a head full of hair and she did not have a big nose. I would not have cared anyway. I would have loved her anyway she came out.

Mommy rushed back to Connecticut. I remember mommy laying eyes on her for the first time. It was love at first sight. Mommy even gave her a nickname. I named her Eboni but Mommy called her Honey. Mommy did not want her out of her sight. Mommy did not even want Eboni's father to spend time with her. I remember times when I would bring Eboni over to see her other side of the family, and mommy would come to where we were and take Eboni. I felt helpless, like I had no control over my child. I remember Eboni spending some time with her grandfather, Jack's dad, and mommy would go to his house and demand that he give the baby to her.

Mommy was so possessive over Eboni. She took very good care of her and made sure I did too. I loved my baby so much. I loved life now. I had something to look forward to every day when I opened my eyes. She was so beautiful. I could not believe how blessed I was. Life became happy again. I should have known that it would not last. Every time I would find joy, it would always come crashing back down to unhappiness.

One day, Mommy announced that we would be moving to North Carolina. I did not understand why she would want to move there. We had no family there at all. But "he" did. This move would become 4 ½ years of hell. I could not imagine life without Jack. How would I live without Jack? How would he see his baby? I thought my life was over. I recall thinking, oh my God, help me LORD.

Chapter 3

On our way to North Carolina. My baby didn't even get to spend her first birthday with her father. We stopped in New Jersey to pick up my sister and say our goodbyes to my daddy and other family members. That was the longest ride of my life. I cried all the way there. All I could think of was the last image I had of Jack, sitting on the curb waving at us and crying as we drove away.

Once we arrived on North Carolina soil, that bastard turned around and looked at us and said "YOU ARE IN MY TERRITORY NOW." The look on his face was smug and sinister. It was that dreaded smile he gets whenever things worked out the way he wanted them to.

We were to live with his parents until Mommy found a place. Mommy would stay with him and his brothers. This would be the first time I would see a dirt road. I never even knew they still existed. We were dropped off with strangers. My eldest sister and I shared a room and my baby sister would share a room with his parents. I did not understand why she couldn't share a room with us. I would later find out why. I remember thinking, this can't be my life.

That very first morning we woke up to two very elderly people staring at us. My sister and I looked at one another and we screamed. It felt like we were in the Twilight Zone. I kept thinking, this is not real. We are going to wake up and be back in Connecticut.

We stayed there for about three months. I hated everything about North Carolina. I hated the smells of the animals, the roads, the snakes, the ditches, and the weather. I even hated the people. I was so depressed. I kept my baby close to me. I wanted to take my baby and my sisters and run as far as I could away from that dreadful place. If mommy wanted to stay then let her stay. I wanted out of that shit hole. And it smelled like shit all the time. I especially hated the smell and taste of the water in that house. It would come out brown; even when you placed it in the refrigerator, it turned the water pitchers brown. It turned our clothes brown. We had to hold our noses to bathe. We drowned our clothes and our bodies in lotion and perfume. I used to think, it can't get any worse than this, or so I thought. But, it got worse, so much worse.

Mommy found a place so we moved but ironically, my baby sister did not come with us. Mommy said she did not want to uproot her from the school she was in, so she had to stay with his family. I was so angry and confused. His mother hated me and she had no problem showing it. There was a time when her granddaughter kept bullying my baby sister, so I confronted her and I let her know that if she bothered my sister again, I was going to hurt her badly. She told 'his" mom, who was her grandma. So, she wanted us to meet so we could hash out our differences. Little did I know she had a plan. She planned to intimidate and scare me.

As we talked, I guess she did not like my responses to her questions and suggestions so she slowly got up and went into her room and grabbed a gun. She walked back into the room with it and threatened me with it. I don't know where I got the courage from, but I looked her in the eye and asked her what she thought she was going to do with it, and I laughed as I said it. I know now that I was staring into the face of a purely evil woman who practiced dark magic. But GOD HAD ME protected and covered. I had not one ounce of fear at that moment. She was so damn mad. She actually feared me because her eyes became wide and she hurriedly put the gun away. I believe she saw the protection of GOD all over me. Thank GOD!

Now I began to understand where "he" got his evilness from. He was born from evil. My sister finally came home to stay with us and she had so many weird stories to tell us about what she had witnessed in that house. All evil.

So many weird things began to happen around our home. Mysterious dogs appeared out of nowhere like they had to protect us. His mom convinced mommy the dogs were evil and that mommy should hurt them so they would leave, and that's what mommy did. But mommy regretted what she did afterward.

We had two driveways to get into our front yard. A dog was lying in each driveway and never allowed that evil woman to get into our yard, and she was so afraid of those dogs. The dogs even knew something was not quite right about that woman. That's when she talked my mom into moving into a trailer on her land. So, we moved onto her land, much to my dismay. But once again, two more dogs appeared and would lay at our front door. The dogs would not allow her to enter our home. They were always watching and in attack mode, but only against her and "him." One day the dogs were gone. We later found out that she poisoned the dogs.

Many weird things happened in that trailer, things that we could not understand or explain. Like the black mushrooms growing out the walls, the phantom snake, and the violence.

One time he tried to choke me yet again, for absolutely no reason at all, as I was coming in from my date with my new boyfriend. I had had it at that point and I left and moved in with my eldest sister. She had gotten married at the age of 15 and mommy signed the papers giving her permission. But this time I made sure my baby sister was close and with me. So, basically my 15-year-old sister was taking care of us along with my baby in a one-bedroom apartment.

At this time I had a boyfriend with whom I would eventually conceive my second child. He treated me very well. More importantly, he accepted Eboni. He had to because she was a part of me. I never heard from her father while we were in North Carolina. But I thought of him often. I became very promiscuous. I slept around a lot. It's like I could not be with my first love so I didn't care about anyone or anything other than my baby, my siblings, and my mom.

My relationship with my second child's father was good until I messed it up. I didn't treat him like he should have been treated. I believe he knew I was cheating on him, and I believe he was cheating as well.

I got pregnant with my second child at the age of 17. So, here I was pregnant again. Mommy was angry but not as angry as she was the first time I became pregnant. I believe the difference this time was the man I had gotten pregnant by.

I had Natasha on Feb. 24, 1991. My labor was hard, long, intense, and painful. I was in labor for three long days. She was 7 pounds. So chunky with beautiful brown skin and a head full of thick, dark, curly hair. A little while after Tasha was born, her father and I parted ways, but he did not neglect his responsibilities as a father. He provided for her and spent quality time with her.

Mommy took me out of school because all I was doing was fighting constantly anyway. I continued to party and continued having sex. I was lonely so I used sex to make me feel wanted and special.

So, by the end of 1991 I had two daughters. Trouble stirred up again. At this time my sister had gotten a divorce and gone to Job Corp. My baby sister started sneaking out of the house. One particular evening my daughter's father came over to visit Tasha and he said he had seen my sister walking down the road. I told him it could not be her because she was upstairs listening to her music, and besides, she would not be walking down that long, dark road all alone. I went upstairs to check on her and she was not there but her window was open. She had jumped out the second-floor window. The police began looking for her, and my mom had to report her as a runaway. My daughter's father and I drove around everywhere looking for her but we couldn't find her.

A few days later there was a knock at the door. My eldest sister was in Job Corp at this time. My mom opened the door and there was Keyonna thank God, but she was not alone. There were two police officers and a DCF worker. I could not understand what they were here for until they said the words I needed to hear, but I also dreaded hearing. Those were words I needed to hear because it meant "he" would be out of our lives. But, I dreaded hearing the words because of what the words would mean.

All three of them entered our home and said that we were being taken into foster care because of "him." When I looked at my sister, she looked so afraid and tired. I was angry with her for having me and mommy worrying about her. But, when I found out the reason, I broke down. "He" was molesting her and making her do disgusting things to him. My heart broke into pieces because I hadn't protected her. I blamed myself for years afterward, and still do to this very day. How could I not know? I made sure that when I left the house he was not there, and I thought he was at work. But he wasn't at work. I found out that he was watching the house, waiting for me to leave so he could go in there and hurt her over and over again, and she never told me or mommy.

We were taken into separate rooms and questioned. We were told to pack clothes as we were being taken to a foster home. They allowed me to take my two babies with me. But when they told me that my sister could not go with us, that she would go to a different foster home, I felt a pain that would go straight to my heart.

When we were in foster care I had no contact with mommy or Keyonna. We were only there for about a week but it felt like so much longer. All kinds of thoughts ran through my head. I wanted my mom, and I wanted my sisters. I couldn't sleep or eat. I just held my babies close to me. I was afraid they would be snatched from me. I remember making a plan in my head. I would kill anyone who tried to take my babies.

We eventually got to go back home to mommy with stipulations of course. Mommy found a wonderful lawyer because they did not want us to go back home. God sent us a miracle because that woman was exactly what and who we needed. I know she was sent by God. I can prove that she was sent by God. Her retainer fee was pretty expensive. Mommy had nowhere near that amount at that time. I would later find out mommy prayed so hard the night before she sought out a lawyer. The next morning there were two $500 checks in the mailbox. Mommy thought they were fake but she stepped out on faith and took the checks to the bank and the checks turned out to be real, legitimate checks.

When Mommy went to the office to meet the lawyer she listened to mommy and agreed to take the case for a fee of $1,000 and she said that mommy could pay her the rest at a later date. Nobody but God.

The day we were to be reunited I ended up in the hospital and placed into intensive care. The foster care system had failed to provide me with the proper medication for my asthma, even though I kept pleading with them that I needed it. I suffered in silence but God gave me the breath and air I needed until I got to that hospital. I was not going to leave my babies alone in that foster home. Once I was reunited with my baby sister, then I went into the hospital. Not realizing that I could have died. God healed me and brought me home healthy and alive.

I remember sitting on the couch. It was so peaceful. I had never felt this peace ever. In the Bible, it says that God will give you peace that surpasses all understanding. At that time God truly gave me that peace. It felt like I could exhale, and I felt so wonderful. I cannot recall if I was dreaming or awoke this one particular afternoon. To this day, I don't know if it was a dream or if I was fully awake. But, I remember seeing blood seeping from every corner in that living room. The blood was falling all over my body, even in my hair. It smelled so sweet like fresh flowers. I began to rub the blood into my skin as if it was a lotion. I would then smell my hands, inhaling the fragrance. I had never experienced anything like it. I have never felt that type of peace since that day.

So, we were home trying to enjoy life. "He" went to jail for a short while and was ordered to stay at least 1500 feet away from us. So, you know what mommy did? She met him at a distance. He could not come to her so she went to him. Life became so much more peaceful without him in our lives.

I ended up meeting someone else. We were just having a little fun, if you know what I mean. There was never a relationship between us. But guess what? Yup, I got pregnant again. Pregnant with my third child.

One evening mommy came home after being with "him." Something was a little off. Mommy was not acting like herself. She told us to pack up whatever clothes we could and whatever was important to us. Mommy said we were going back to Connecticut in the morning. The year was 1992. I remember it being so hot that day. I was so happy to hear those words come from mommy. I was seven months pregnant with my third child. I never even told her father, at first. I just wanted to get away from that state. I hated taking Tasha away from her father, but we had to do what we had to do for our safety.

Mommy gave everything away but put the most important stuff in storage. Tasha's father took us to the bus station to purchase our tickets-me, mommy, my baby sister, and my two babies. And during the whole ride back, all I could think about was reuniting with Jack.

Chapter 4

We made it safely back to Connecticut. The first person we saw when we got off the bus was my aunt. I can remember my heart swelling and bursting with love seeing her, and being back in Connecticut again.

We went to her house, showered and changed. We caught up on old times. I was so happy at that moment. I was even happier when I saw my cousin and met her daughter for the first time. My mom and my aunt started making plans. Mom and I were under the impression that we would stay with them until we got on our feet but we were wrong. She showed us to the nearest shelter where we could stay. I was shocked and surprised by this. My feelings were so hurt. A foster home and now a shelter? This couldn't be happening. But it happened. We went to a shelter.

At that time Jack was not in Connecticut. He was in South Carolina in prison. I also would find out that he had a son. I was a little upset. Didn't I have the nerve, knowing I had two (nearly three since I was pregnant at the time) more children than he did? I stayed there with my babies, my mommy, and my sister. I hated it and I asked my cousin if me and my babies could stay at her place. She agreed and I was so happy. I ended up staying there for about two months.

We found a place and lo and behold on the day we were to move in, I went into labor. I had Amber on October 27, 1992. Another beautiful, chunky girl, weighing 7 pounds and 6 ounces. Her delivery was fast and quick.

Mommy found a job and my eldest sister joined us in Connecticut. I remember moving into this one particular apartment. Weird things began to happen. I don't want to spook you. I don't want my story to be about haunted houses and ghosts, but this was my life, and it's true. I must tell it all. It will all make sense in the end or maybe not; only God and time will tell.

My baby girl Amber would get up in the middle of the night. I would find her singing and talking to people. But I never saw the people, only she did. My mom would pray.

The next person that I met who would become my fourth daughter's father moved in with us. We had a lot of fun together. I became pregnant when Amber was only six months old. I chose to terminate the pregnancy, a mistake I regret to this very day.

Right before Amber turned one, we received some very devastating news that my father had passed away. I can still remember that awful phone call we received from his sister, my aunt. It was like the wind was knocked out of me. Keyonna had just spent the summer with him. The day was October 3, 1993. I will never forget that day. I had so many regrets. I should have spent more time with him, should have talked to him more, should have written letters. Now it was too late.

My eldest sister was in the National Guard at this time in South Carolina, and she flew home immediately. The drive to New Jersey seemed to take forever. Daddy's funeral was beautiful. A lot of people came to pay their respects. I was in a daze. There were only four things that stuck out in my mind that day at the funeral. My daddy laying there and the fact that I would never have another conversation with him again; my uncle being ushered down the aisle walking slowly to see his brother lying there dead; the police on both sides of my uncle who was in prison at the time. The state had allowed him out to see his brother one last time; and hearing the shackles that were attached to his arms and legs. My sister fell on his casket and my uncle had to pick her up. My grandfather, my mom's dad, standing up at the back of the church with his head bowed. I felt so much hurt, shame, guilt, and regret. My daddy, my hero, was gone.

My mom called me Fertile Myrtle because I got pregnant again. But the dad and I broke up before she was born. Then I received the best news in the world. Jack was back in Connecticut. He was looking for me and we found each other. I was three months pregnant with someone else's child but that didn't matter to him. He wanted me and I wanted him.

Theresa was born on June 29, 1995. My chunky, round-faced baby girl. She was another 7 pound beautiful baby. Here I was, with four daughters at the age of 21. I couldn't be happier. I started to notice the more babies I had, the happier I would become. So, I did just that. I had more children. Life was good and the family was getting along very well. Mommy was working and my sister was working. Keyonna had gone back to our old church and she was finally happy. I guess the therapy and church helped her. Thank God for healing.

So we decided to move once again but within the same city. This townhouse was a huge 6-bedroom, with two bathrooms and three floors. We were happy there in the beginning. That is, until strange things began to happen there as well. It was as if something bad was following us. My mom and my sister began to hear and see strange things. I remember not worrying too much about it. My mom never wanted to sleep upstairs on the third floor alone. Mommy would always come downstairs and sneak one of my daughters upstairs with her which was usually Amber. I had no problem with it until Amber started seeing things and talking to ghosts or spirits.

One particular evening my mom caught her sitting up in her bed talking to someone. Mommy didn't disturb her conversation at that point but she listened. Amber asked the spirit what he was doing in Mommy's room at that time of night. He asked Amber to take his hand and come with him. It was at that point that mommy asked Amber who was she talking to. Amber described the man as having on dirty white sneakers, dirty blue jeans, a T-shirt, and a hat on. But he disappeared when he heard mommy's voice. It was at this point that I no longer wanted the girls to sleep on the third floor.

But mommy would continue to sneak them upstairs whenever I fell asleep or had my door closed. Another strange thing Amber witnessed was dirty water in the bathtub which was odd because there was no water in the tub, and she was the only one who could see it.

One night my baby sister got up to use the bathroom and found my mom downstairs on the second floor in the bed with the girls. Mommy was fast asleep. Keyonna looked back in on mommy after relieving herself and saw mommy's arm being slowly lifted as she was sleeping. It was as if someone was lifting her arm in the air. My sister began to pray and woke mom up to tell her what she had just witnessed. This only scared mommy even more.

One evening one of my daughters was using the second-floor bathroom so Jack had to use the third-floor bathroom. After about ten minutes of him being up there, I could hear him running rapidly back down the stairs. He hopped back in the bed behind me saying he had seen something. He never did reveal to me at that time what he saw. It would be years later when he would finally open up to me. He said he saw a dark shadow in the bathroom with him. All he could remember was that it was tall and had on black in the shape of a man.

And finally, it would be my turn. I remember earlier that day and night I had been drinking and playing cards at Jack's family house. I had gotten in pretty late and I was very intoxicated. I fell asleep as soon as my head hit the pillow. I don't remember how long I was asleep when all of a sudden I heard a voice whisper in my ear to go upstairs and wake up my mother. It was so clear. I immediately sat up and placed my feet on the floor as I looked up at the stairs that faced my room. I asked God a question. I asked Him if I had to, as I was afraid. I got up anyway and hurried up the stairs. As I proceeded to climb the stairs, I could hear my mom murmuring or moaning. I can't remember which. As I entered her room, the only words that I could utter out my mouth was "Mom, that thing got you again, doesn't it?" My mom immediately opened her eyes, looked at me, and said , "Yeah." As I looked at her and she looked at me, I noticed her skin was pale white. I could not believe my eyes.

My uncle and his family moved in with us for a little while. Things began to settle down. They also brought with them one of the meanest dogs I ever came in contact with. They had to keep the dog upstairs in the room. They were very strange people. My three cousins were not allowed out of the room unless it was time to eat and they only ate pasta. From what I could see, they were never even allowed to eat candy or snacks. They hardly talked. But they were family and we made it work.

My uncle was retired from the military. He seemed to be so controlling over them. They acted as if they were afraid of him. I believed he liked it. My uncle tried to control our house as well and put fear in our hearts, but me and my sisters were not having it. After all the hell we had been through previously with "him" there was absolutely no way we were going to allow my uncle to come into our house and take over it and us.

They moved out a few months later. My eldest sister was pregnant. It was 1995. The one person who everyone thought would never have a baby because she was mean, selfish, stingy, and loved to run the streets. But she had her baby. She named her Tiranee. I had the honor of being there to witness her birth. But my sister had a few complications and had to get a C-section. But when she came out of the surgery, I was right there to see my niece. She was beautiful and yes, chunky, just like mine were.

We moved out of that house about a year after my uncle and his family moved out. We received more good news that my baby sister was getting married. We were all so happy. She got married at the age of 17, to a pastor's kid. Her wedding was beautiful. Amber would be the flower girl and I would be one of the bridesmaids. Nisha was the maid of honor.

And guess what else? I was a pregnant bridesmaid. Yes, I was pregnant again with Jack's baby. This made baby number five. I was kind of afraid to have this child. I even thought about getting an abortion but I could not do it. I gave birth to a 7-pound baby boy. Finally a boy after four girls. He was born on May 16, 1997. I named him Javon Lee. I gave him the name Lee after my father. I was proud to give him my father's name. His hair was beautiful. I loved to brush it and run my fingers through it.

After a few months, I got pregnant again. At this point, I became secretly depressed. I hid it so well from everyone. I started to talk down to myself. I felt embarrassed about being pregnant again. I started to think about what everyone would say. I started to feel I could not do anything right but have babies. I had no job, things were not going well with Jack because he had a drug addiction. So here I was with five kids, pregnant with my sixth, with no job, and a man who used drugs and did not have a job himself. We were barely surviving and living off the state. But God was there in the midst even though I couldn't see or feel Him. But I remembered that mommy had taught me the power of prayer. I prayed and God always provided. I couldn't give up. I had to take care of my kids. No one knew how unhappy I was but God. No one knew how many nights I cried.

I remember one of the few times I went to get my hair done, I had a conversation with the hairstylist. I knew her well because she was Keyonna's sister-in-law. She was washing my hair and she suddenly stopped. I remember exactly what she said. She said to me "Gilly, God said don't be ashamed of your children. God gave you those children. You need not be ashamed of them."

You see, it was not that I was ashamed of my kids because I wasn't. I was ashamed of the fact that I kept having baby after baby without having anything to give them. I was so depressed with my sixth pregnancy. But God got me through it. Dashawn Otis was born on September 16, 1998, weighing 6 pounds. He was a little skinny thing but oh so handsome. Yes, I gave him my daddy's middle name. I was proud to give another son my dad's name.

I got a job in 1999. I worked at a motel as a motel clerk. I loved my job. This is where I met my best friend Sylvia, who I can say to this day is still my best friend. We got along so well. I love this woman.

The following year while sitting in the church we both belonged to at this time, The Temple Of Faith, Keyonna would become a minister. An amazing Apostle and First Lady who we were under, and who taught me so much. I will forever be grateful to God for them.

One Sunday afternoon mommy went up to the altar. Mommy was slain in the spirit which is a term we Christian Pentecostals use. Mommy was on the floor for quite some time. I remember the Usher tapping me on the shoulder telling me she thought something was wrong with mommy. I proceeded to tell the Usher to get my other sister's attention to let her know. I was afraid. All three of us were in church this particular Sunday, which was odd.

They got mommy up off the floor and she was confused and

in a daze. We rushed her to the hospital. We found out that she had had 8 TIAs, which means she'd had 8 mini-strokes. Thank God Mommy recovered with no problems, or so we thought. That was the beginning of many strokes and a decline in her health.

In 1999, I found out I was pregnant yet again with my seventh child. Yes pregnant again, but I was happy because I knew no one could take my babies away. They were my miracles, my accomplishments; my babies loved me and I loved them. I hated to let them out of my sight. I never even wanted them to go outside to play without my watchful eye. I had so much anxiety. Always thinking someone was going to snatch them away from me.

My baby sister and I were both pregnant at the same time; me with my seventh and her with her first.

Tamar Elijah was born on March 13, 2000. He was a whopping almost 9-pound baby boy. He was so handsome and beyond chunky. So much so that mommy gave him the nickname Chunky. I continued working while mommy watched the kids for me. She would spend the weekends at her sister's house to unwind and relax after watching the kids all week.

Now, this whole time I must tell you that Jack and mommy argued every day. She still hated him even after all these years. I was always the referee and the peacekeeper. It was so stressful. Jack was constantly in the streets, getting high, back and forth to jail every couple of months. Yet I continued to do what I had to do for my kids, all while still battling asthma. But, I never gave up on Jack. I kept believing he was going to change. I prayed for myself a lot. He was always getting into trouble. Every time he would go to jail, I would send money to him like a fool. I would pay people to give me a ride to the prisons to see him. I had so much love for this man. In my silly mind, I used to think I might as well deal with him because who else is going to want a woman with 7 kids? It was nobody but God, my kids, and my mommy who gave me the strength to keep going.

My sister gave birth to her baby boy on April 9, 2000. She named him Ezakah. I was happy to be an aunt for the second time. It was around this time that mommy started acting a little weird to me. I could not place my finger on it at that time. But it would be revealed.

I remember one beautiful fall day I was doing some Spring cleaning and there was suddenly a knock at the front door. When I opened the door a police officer was standing there with a Caucasian lady. I proceeded to ask them "How can I help you?" THE LADY TOLD ME SHE WAS A DCF WORKER. She told me there was a complaint that I was not feeding my children, or sending them to school; that I was allowing them to be outside in the wee hours of the morning. There was also a complaint that I had no food in my house. I was so angry and afraid that they would try to take my children from me, even though all the accusations were false.

My thoughts immediately went to my mom's side of the family, because I knew my father's side of the family would not make these accusations. I had not been in touch with them for years. My mom assured me it was not them, but someone else whom I will not reveal.

At the same time I was speaking to this woman and trying to defend myself against these horrible accusations, there were DCF workers at my kids school speaking to and questioning them. I was not aware of that until after they arrived home from school that day. At this time my children were still young. The DCF worker told me that I needed a little more food in my refrigerator, and that they would be back at the end of the day with a decision. True to their word they returned that day. My freezer and refrigerator as well as my cabinets were completely stocked. My house was spotless. The worker told me that all the accusations were unfounded and that they were closing my case that very day. God's grace and mercy showed up again.

At the end of 2000, we found out that grandpa was sick. Mommy decided to leave Connecticut to go to New Jersey and help care for her father. Grandpa had cancer. Mommy stayed at grandma and grandpa's house to care for him. Several months later grandpa would succumb to his illness. He died on September 28, 2001.

Mommy came back home. I would lose my job in 2001 because the motel was bought out by another company, and they wanted us to take a pay cut. We refused and left. Then lo and behold, this is when I found out I was pregnant again with my 8th child. I collected unemployment for a short period. But by the grace of God before my unemployment ran out I would find another job.

I started working at a very popular hotel. The pay was good and I loved the job. This is where I would meet a powerful woman of God. She taught me so much. She always encouraged me and never made me feel like I had nothing to offer. She explained to me that I needed to watch what I released out of my mouth. That's when I learned to start speaking positively and not always negatively. She helped me in so many ways. She had the Word of God in her and she had so much wisdom. Susan Williams demanded her respect and she got it. So here I was with two powerful friends in my life. I loved and respected them both. They were like night and day, but one thing they had in common was their love for God and their church.

Once again, my sister was pregnant as well with her second child. We would later find out that she was blessed with twins. My baby was born on March 9, 2002. Jada Nicole was born weighing 7 pounds, and my sister Keyonna was there with me for her birth because Jack was in jail yet again. I decided to give her my middle name, Nicole. Keyonna would have the twins about two months later. She was blessed with a boy and a girl. They were fraternal twins, Shaniah and Josiah.

About two weeks after Jada was born, I received a weird call from one of my aunts. She asked me how was my daughter's hair? I found it odd as she had just left my house one hour before that. My sister came by later that day to perm my mom's hair. When my sister arrived to do mommy's hair, it looked like mommy's hair was frozen to her scalp. I remember my sister screaming and praying. She started to speak in tongues over my mom's hair. My sister ran downstairs to her car to get the Holy Oil, then she ran back up the stairs and poured the oil all over mommy's hair, all the while praying to God. I began to put two and two together. I believed my aunt tried to do something to my daughter's hair, but it happened to mommy instead. Makes you wonder right? YES, ME TOO. I did not understand it then but I do now. The prayer and oil worked because mommy's hair would become beautiful and silky again. I cannot and will not make this stuff up. It's true, my truth.

In 2003, my eldest sister would get married for the second time. The wedding was beautiful. I was at the wedding. Keyonna was the photographer. So, here I go again, always the bridesmaid but never the bride. Jack was in jail once again and could not attend the wedding.

Chapter 5

In mid-2004 my baby sister decided to make a drastic decision. Keyonna moved to Pennsylvania with her husband to open their church. Mommy went with her to help with the children. I couldn't believe mommy was leaving me. Who would be there to help me with my children? Was I being selfish? Absolutely. I did not want mommy to leave me. I did not want my sister to leave me either. I had so many questions, too. Why now? Just when I thought things were starting to look up for me, they just up and left me. But just when I thought that I was alone Sylvia stepped in. She was not only my best friend, she was my backbone. Sylvia helped me style my girl's hair, wash their clothes, and even with cooking meals. I don't know what I would have done without her.

Keyonna named her church S.H.R.E.D. Ministries. But, my sister was going through some things we did not know about at that time. She chose to suffer in silence.

I remember visiting her one time in Pennsylvania. I knew something wasn't right but I could not pinpoint the problem. I dared not question her because she was a Pastor. What could I possibly say to her? How could I, a sinner, encourage her or give her advice?

Keyonna called me one afternoon while I was at work to inform me that she could not find mommy. She said mommy had walked to the store and had not returned after an hour. I was so worried. I prayed that she would be found. Thank God, Keyonna found her. How could Mommy get lost on a walk that she took almost every day? We did not know then that this would not be the last time that she would get lost.

In 2005, we decided to give mommy a well-deserved surprise birthday party. My sisters and I planned a 70s birthday theme for her. Keyonna, mommy, her kids, and her husband traveled from Pennsylvania as we were having the party in Connecticut. Only 6 of mommy's 13 siblings showed up. The party still turned out to be perfect. Mommy had a wonderful time. People stood and paid tribute to her with beautiful words and speeches. Her grandchildren gave her flowers. Mommy received money and beautiful gifts. Oh, and I forgot to mention that I was pregnant again at the time of the party. Eight months pregnant. Yup, eight months pregnant with my ninth child.

Jayden Timothy was born on Jan, 3, 2006. He weighed 6 pounds. Jayden was so yellow that I kind of wondered if this was my baby. He looked like a mixed child. But, he was my "Jorge" as mommy started to call him.

Mommy, my sister and her husband, and my nieces and nephews moved back to Connecticut in 2006. Mommy would not stay long though. Her siblings and her mother talked her into moving back to New Jersey to help out with grandma so she wouldn't be alone since grandpa was no longer there. Being the person she was, mommy helped out anyone she could. Mommy, the person who could never say no to anyone. I could not understand why out of 13 siblings she would have to be the one to go. There were at least five of her siblings already living in New Jersey who could have moved in with grandma, and there was also a host of grandchildren. Grandma had three of her siblings there as well.

Chapter 6

Mommy was now in New Jersey. That's when weird things started to happen and mommy began to change. At this time, Keyonna and Nisha took over mommy's Power of Attorney and became her conservators since she had had the strokes. We really made a conscious and smart decision by doing so. The decision also came by the grace of God. God will always give you warnings before destruction. At this time, mommy was receiving money from disability. Keyonna would also send her money whenever mommy needed it. But mommy seemed to need money too frequently. Every week mommy would call fussing that she needed more money. It would be at least two to three hundred dollars a week. We could not understand it since she had everything she needed. Keyonna would send it anyway, but she would keep every single receipt of every MoneyGram that she would send to mommy. She would say later that something told her to keep the receipts. I'm so glad she did because they would come in handy later.

I remember being home one day on my day off and I received a disturbing phone call from my grandmother. My grandmother asked me if something was wrong with my mother, if she was crazy. I remember two of my aunts asking me the same thing nine years earlier. My grandmother then proceeded to tell me to come and get mommy. And go get her we did, the very next day.

I remember being angry. My mom had dropped everything

and put her life on hold to help grandma, for grandma to then turn around and call her crazy and tell us to come get her.

My sister Nisha drove and me and my best friend Sylvia were passengers. When we arrived there was so much tension in the air. I felt uncomfortable being in that house. There was evil there and I knew something was not quite right. Yes, I wanted my mom out of there immediately. I did not want her there if she was not welcome anymore.

What would happen next confused and angered me even more as my sister and mommy packed her things. My grandma became angry and she told my sister to get my mom out of her house. My sister said, "Gladly, no problem!" Nisha began to throw all of mommy's belongings in trash bags so we could hurry up and just get the hell out of there.

As we walked out the door, I will never forget the words that came out of my grandmother's mouth. She said to us "Never bring her back here." I turned around in utter shock and anger. I could not believe what she had said. She said it with so much anger and hatred. I would never forget the look in her eyes either. I remember the hurt in my mommy's eyes when she heard those words. I vowed that they would never hurt my mom again.

The ride on the way back home was eerily quiet until my sister started asking questions. My sister was even angrier than I was. She had no problem showing her anger. What I wanted to know was why she wanted my mom out of her house, and why was she so angry about it? What had mommy done or said? There were so many unanswered questions and mommy wasn't talking.

It was as if she did not want us to know the "whys;" like she didn't want to taint our minds against them. Mommy was hiding something, but we were determined to find out what had happened while mommy was in New Jersey. What had they done to our once loving, sweet, kind-hearted mother? But we would not get answers to our questions, at least not from mommy.

So, now we are back in Connecticut with mommy and she is living with me. And guess what? I'm pregnant again with baby number 10. I continued to work and mommy watched the children for me. This was a difficult pregnancy. My diabetes was out of control as well as my asthma. But, I still worked and pushed myself. Jack was still out in the streets getting high and drinking. Thank God for my mother. She made sure the kids were taken care of while I worked.

I remember one night in Jan. of 2007, I would hear something that would haunt me for years to come. I heard that my daughter had been raped over and over and over again by a close family members' of Jack. I was devastated. I was angry, confused, ashamed, and sad. I hurt for my daughter. This can't be happening again. Not again. I had failed to protect my daughter, just like I had failed to protect my sister. I didn't know what to do. Do I report this and let my daughter Theresa get before a judge and relive this all over again? Do I report this and possibly have all of my children taken from me just like when it had happened in North Carolina? I hated that he had done this to my child, and I hated myself for not knowing. How does she move forward from this? But, I made one of the worst mistakes I could have made. I left the decision up to her, a 14-year-old child because I didn't know how to handle it. I felt like that 9-year-old little girl all over again when the gun was put to my head. I held in the aching in my heart for my child. I thought if I just prayed she would be alright, not knowing that I would scar my child. There was so much turmoil in my head. I hated myself.

I remember the day I went to the hospital and I was admitted because I was in labor. Mommy and two of my other children came to visit me, Theresa and Amber. This was a long labor. So mommy and the girls decided to leave because they were going to a church service. As soon as they left and walked down the hallway, I suddenly felt the baby's head start to push out of me. I yelled for them to come back and get the doctor. I was so happy they did not leave and they were able to see the birth of Teonna Lashwan Costin. It was February 25, 2007. But an emergency arose during labor and I kept pushing when they told me to stop. I tried my hardest to stop pushing but I couldn't. By not following the doctor's instructions, I broke her clavicle, which means I broke her collarbone. I felt so guilty and afraid. But as it turned out, the doctor said the injury would heal itself, and thank God it did after only one week. And, oh my goodness she was the chubbiest thing with a head full of curly hair. She weighed almost 8 pounds and looked Asian, as she still does to this very day.

Chapter 7

I remember one awful, horrible day like it was yesterday. It was about three weeks after Teonna was born. Me and mommy were arguing about Jack as usual, because she still hated him with a passion. Like a fool, I was defending him yet again. My sister came over and mommy marched upstairs still angry with me. My sister Nisha decided to go and get some lunch. I remember mommy being so mad that she did not want any lunch. So, my sister and I ate lunch. My eldest daughter and her friend had just walked through the door after getting out of school. My daughter went upstairs to put her things away. I remember her yelling my name and my sister's name. My sister jumped up and flew up the stairs taking them two at a time. I immediately dialed 911. It was as if I already knew what had happened. It happened so quickly. Mommy was only upstairs for about 40 minutes. After talking to the 911 operator I ran up the stairs.

Mommy was just lying there on the floor. She could not speak or move. I felt so helpless. I felt so much fear. When the paramedics arrived, I rode in the ambulance with mommy. Nisha drove her car and met us there. I remember not wanting to take that ride. I was afraid she was going to die and I would have to witness it.

When we arrived, Nisha was already there. The doctors started working on mommy and she was fighting them. They were trying to intubate her but she was putting up a fight. I remember standing there in the middle of the floor in a daze, in disbelief. Can this be happening? Is my mother lying there with her mouth slightly twisted? I just stood there shaking and crying. My sister looked back at me, yelling my name, but I could not hear her. All I could see was that her mouth was moving. She shook me and then I heard her. She told me to go outside and get myself together; that I was no good for mommy right then. I turned and ran outside and sat on a bench, still in a daze.

I don't even know how I managed to call Keyonna. Keyonna was already at the hospital because she worked there. I explained to her what had happened. Keyonna got to the ER in 5 minutes. She ran up to me asking me what room mommy was in, but I couldn't talk. I couldn't get the words out of my mouth. Keyonna just left me and went to go find mommy. I didn't want to call mommy's sisters but I knew I had to. They were there in 20 minutes. It was confirmed that mommy had had a massive stroke which had placed her in a coma. She would be in a coma for at least two weeks. This is when some trouble started that would last for years to come, even to this very day.

My grandmother arrived a day or two later with all but three of mommy's other siblings. I remember the day the rest of the family arrived. I was the only one at the hospital. I was waiting for Nisha and Keyonna to arrive, so I was alone with the rest of the family. We were all in the family waiting room.

I noticed my grandmother looking at me with hatred. I tried to ignore her. I was thinking about my mother. She then sspoke up and said to me that we were stealing my mom's money and beating her. I looked up to see who she was talking to. I knew she could not have been referring to me. So, I asked her if she was talking to me? My grandmother said "Yeah, I'm talking to you." So to avoid any conflict, I walked out of that room and went into the hallway.

I called my sister Keyonna first, then I called Nisha to let them know what was going on. but Nisha didn't answer. Keyonna was so angry. I could not believe how fast she arrived at the hospital. When Keyonna arrived we both went back into the room together.

Keyonna proceeded to tell them all that if they had any questions about mommy's money to ask her because she had control over the money, not me. My grandma felt bold enough to speak up, I guess because she was surrounded by all her children. She walked up to my sister, got in her face and told her that she had been stealing her daughter's money. I remember Keyonna asking her to kindly back up out of her face because she was in her space. My grandma did not budge, so Keyonna stood up to repeat herself. Then there was pandemonium.

My aunt tried to swing on my sister but I grabbed her arm and slightly nudged her and she tumbled into a lamp. My other aunts all tried to come at us, and a few tried to break us apart. In the middle of all this, my sister Nisha walked past the glass window on her way to my mom's room and she stopped, backed up, and ran into the room. Nisha put me and Keyonna behind her and and told them if they took one more step near us she was going to cut their throats.

I started to hyperventilate and became short of breath. One of my aunts noticed and yelled to get a pump and a doctor. Keyonna yelled out, "Don't you touch her! I will take care of her!" Keyonna grabbed my pump and told me to open my mouth, then she sprayed the medicine into my mouth.

Five seconds later I heard heavy footsteps running down the hall toward us. It was the police. Unbeknownst to us, they had been watching everything on camera. Once the police calmed everyone down and got the situation under control, the Supervisor made an announcement. He told everyone if they were not Darlene's children, husband, or son-in-law, they had to leave. My grandma was angry and told the police that she was the mother and she was not leaving. The Officer told her she was leaving right along with the rest of them or they were going to jail. They left but not before offering me money. I knew what it would mean if I allowed that money to touch my hands, so I refused and did not touch it.

Chapter 8

Mommy survived the stroke but she had a long way to go to recover. We were praying a lot and spent a lot of time at the hospital. We spent so many hours with Mommy, and frequently meeting with doctors. My baby was not even a month old yet. I had to rely on my oldest daughters to look after the younger kids as they were still teenagers themselves. Of course, Jack was not around enough to look after the children. I could not even count on him in the darkest moment in my life. That's when the resentment toward him started to set in.

Mommy stayed at Yale Hospital for a little over two months. After those two months, Mommy was moved to Gaylord Rehabilitation Center. She had to learn how to walk and talk all over again. Mommy was so stubborn at times. She wanted to exercise and do speech therapy when she wanted to do it. It was during those times that the staff would call Nisha. The doctors and nurses even gave Nisha a nickname. They called her the Drill Sergeant.

We did physical therapy and speech therapy with mommy. We even had to teach her how to dress. We had to push mommy. She wanted to give up so many times. But she didn't; she kept going. I admired her strength. Mommy had always been a fighter.

Gaylord would become like our second home. We were there every day, and I do mean every day. I spent as much time as possible at home as well. But my daughters Eboni and Natasha were truly the "moms" at this point. We all were stressed out and tired. But God gave us all the strength we needed to keep going. I cried many nights but I hid it from everyone, especially the kids. I was so heartbroken for my mommy. I watched her struggle but I never saw her give up.

Mommy would stay at Gaylord through Mother's Day. I remember bringing all the kids up to see her. All of my nieces and nephews came up as well. Some of her sisters even came up, and we had lunch with her and drew paintings. We even painted angels that we all took home with us. We had such a wonderful time. Mommy was happy to see everyone. That was a good memory.

Mommy came home soon after that day. She went home with Nisha. She continued her physical therapy, speech therapy, and occupational therapy at Nisha's house. Mommy gave the therapists a hard time. She did not want to continue therapy, but we pushed her hard and she fought back with anger, hostility, frustration, and sometimes violence. Mommy was with Nisha for about three months but she came to my house on the weekends when my sister needed a break.

So, in between working and taking care of 10 kids, I was also caring for mommy on the weekends. Mommy slowly began to get better, so Keyonna moved mommy in with her. She was still at my house on the weekends, which I didn't mind. I was just grateful that Mommy was alive and getting better every day. The process was still hard as mommy's personality had changed which was to be expected. I noticed she got angry very easily. She began to hold on to her possessions for dear life, as if someone was going to take them from her. I remember one time when she was lying on my couch, and I went to fix her pillows and found five sharp knives. I was shocked and afraid. I started to wonder if the stroke had taken a little of her mind.

Therapy continued for several months. Doctors' appointments continued and her anger continued, only the anger was getting worse. Anything would set mommy off. If she did not like what we cooked for her meals, it would anger her. If the kids were too loud it would anger her. If she saw Jack in the house it would anger her. No matter how I tried to make her happy and keep her calm it would never last for long. Mommy slowly started to become combative and irate a lot. It started to become very hard to handle her at times. I noticed when I would play some Gospel music that mommy would calm down and immediately go into worship mode. Mommy loved Gospel music. Her favorite artists were James Cleveland, Shirley Caesar, The Williams Brothers, and many more.

Chapter 9

The year was now 2008. Many things happened that year. My baby girl would be born. The very last baby that I would carry in my womb. You see, after the birth of Aniyah Caprice who was born on October 6, weighing 7 pounds, I got a tubal ligation; in simpler terms, I got my tubes tied. I would never have a baby again. I was a mom of 11 beautiful children. Seven girls and four boys.

I had my last baby, but I also became a grandma for the first time. It was too funny. My eldest daughter Eboni was pregnant at the same time. My granddaughter, Ashiya Leshay Williams would be born three months after my baby. I was blessed to be there and see the birth of my first grandchild. Her other grandma Susan was there as well. Ashiya was born on January 25, 2009.

That same year, a few months after Aniyah was born, I would have to stop working at my job after having been there for 6 and a half years. I had to leave my job because of my asthma and also to care for my mother. Mommy was staying with Keyonna as I stated previously, but Keyonna brought mommy over one day to stay for a few days with me while she took a business trip. Let's just say she never came back to get mommy. Mommy stayed with me for many years to come.

I remember one particular weekend there was a church picnic so a few of my children wanted to stay the night at Keyonna's house. The very next morning there was a knock at her door. Lo and behold it was policemen and DCF workers. Yes, it happened again, but this time it was Keyonna and my children happened to be there.

As with my case, the accusations were unfounded, of course, and the case was closed but not before my mom, niece, and nephews were questioned and their bodies examined. The accusations were unbelievable. Someone accused my sister of abusing her children and our mom. She was also accused of neglect on so many levels. We knew who it was at this point. Family can be your worst enemy. My sister was so angry and she wanted revenge. But God would not allow it. You see, our faith and trust in God is what got us through these tough times.

I remember one night my sister called me from a store parking lot. She did not sound like herself. My sister saw the family member that we knew was behind the false accusations. She said she was going to run her over with my car. At first, I thought she was only joking but I soon realized that she was very serious. I had to keep talking to her and giving her the Word of God. I had to remind her of her children, mommy, and the law. I had to pray as I was reminding her of these things. I thank God that He heard my prayers. We had to stay close as a family because we only had each other. We now knew for sure that my mother's side of the family had it out for us and they were not playing fair. We knew they didn't like us but this was getting out of control. The dislike for us had turned into hatred. All we could do at this point was talk amongst ourselves and try to figure out why all the hatred toward us.

Not very long after that my sisters and I received letters in the mail from Probate Court. Who would have thought the accusations toward us could get much worse? The Costins were taking us to the court concerning our mother. They accused us of abusing her, and taking her disability checks. They also accused us of allowing our husbands and boyfriends to beat on her and burn her with cigarettes. To our dismay, they even put the dog into the accusations. They claimed the dog was dangerous to her and he should not be allowed to be near her. They told the judge that we would not allow them to see her. What we could not understand was how they could accuse us of doing these things to her, and in the same breath say that we would not allow them to see her. If you weren't seeing her, then how could you make these ridiculous accusations? After the initial shock, my feelings went from hurt to anger to hate. Every time I thought about the situation, I would become enraged; then I would cry. Like, is this really happening? The family that I thought loved us really did not love us. This upcoming court hearing consumed my mind day and night. My sisters were angry and so were my older children.

I remember the court day like it was yesterday. Me and my sisters, Keyonna's husband, and our Apostle were in attendance. A few of my aunts were in attendance as well. The case was not resolved at this court hearing. I can remember one of my aunts being so angry to the point where I saw pure hatred in her eyes. She became irate at our Apostle. She cursed at him and got in his face and made threats. He looked her straight in her eyes and smiled, which only made her angrier. That exchange did not sit well with Keyonna's husband because our Apostle was his father. So he proceeded to let my aunt know that she better not ever disrespect his father again. My aunt looked like an evil demon, and she acted like one as well. I guess if a person puts their hand into black magic it's not hard to look like or act like a demon. Yes, we knew what they were into. We did not confront them. But what we did do was give it to God. We gave the whole horrible situation to the Lord. In between the next court hearing, at one point we allowed them to visit with mommy and the result was that almost a year later we would end up in court again.

This time we were allowed to bring in character witnesses. So we brought in close friends of ours. It was so bad that they even talked down to our friends and wanted to see their credentials and paperwork if anyone stated that they helped to care for our mother. The whole hearing was a disaster. One of my aunts even went so far as to start an argument with the Court Reporter. The judge asked my mother who she wanted to see. My aunt spoke up and told the judge that my mom could not talk. So the judge decided to ask mommy himself. Mommy told the judge the only one she wanted to see was her mother. I could not understand why my grandmother wanted to see her as she had previously stated to us that she did not want to see her, and to never bring her back to her home.

My grandmother decided to give a speech at the end of the court proceeding. Grandma was doing okay for a while, that is until she started to put us down and say untruthful things and the judge ordered her to sit down and be quiet. So that was the court order. We would allow her mother to visit as long as her request was with at least 48 hours advance notice. We were livid, but this was her mother and she wanted to see her mom so we did not contest the order.

Even with the order she still did not visit for a few months. When she did decide to contact us for a visit we allowed the visit. My aunts were with her but we decided to allow mommy to go anyway. They were to take mommy out to lunch and bring her back at the time we agreed on. Of course, they were late and did not take mommy where they said they were going. Keyonna got in touch with one of them and told them to have mommy back in twenty minutes. They brought mommy back with some kind of wig on her head. I shudder to think of what they did to mommy. I remember taking the wig off my mommy's head as I helped her out of the car. My aunts were in the backseat murmuring under their breath. I wanted to snatch them out of the car and beat the hell out of them. It took all my self-control and God to keep me off them. Nisha came to help me get mommy out of the car but she saw my grandmother and tried to hug her, but my grandma refused to hug her. My grandma had a look of pure hatred in her eyes.

We had a few months of peace with no contact from them and it felt good. We felt we had to protect mommy from her own family, which was so sad. Mommy was our priority even though we knew God had it all under control. But, I can look back now and see that we never fully gave it all to God. That is, not until another court date was soon to come again. They would not stop. They were relentless. But so were we. We just did it differently. We did it with God; we did it with God's strength and trusted in Him. God always gave us warnings before destruction. So before this court hearing me and my children along with my sisters came together in prayer for mommy. We could not understand what they wanted. They did not want the responsibility of caring for her, but they did not want us to have the responsibility of caring for her either. I lost many nights of sleep standing guard on mom's behalf.

I remember this one particular prayer. This prayer was different. This prayer was powerful. Keyonna was late getting there. We did not think that she was going to show. I remember when she walked in, she immediately fell on mommy's lap. Mommy rubbed her baby's head to reassure her all would be well. God showed up to prayer that day and He used my Amber and my niece Tiranee. God revealed to us that He was going to make them so tired to the point of confusion. God did just what He said.

The following day not one of them showed up to the court proceeding. I remember sitting there in front of the judge and him asking us, what do you want me to do? It was like God Himself was sitting there asking this question. I remember looking directly into the judge's eyes and asking him to throw it out. The judge looked at me and said, "Done." He hit the gavel on the desk to emphasize that this was the final order. My God, I was truly grateful to God. Again, God came through on our behalf. I could do nothing but praise Him.

In 2010, I would be tested yet again, but this time it would not be mommy, but my baby girl Aniyah. I remember noticing a slight limp every time Aniyah would walk or run. I took her to see a doctor on two occasions. Both times the doctors assured me that she was fine.

One particular afternoon Amber had taken Aniyah with her to her boyfriend's house. Not soon after, Amber called me and said Aniyah had slipped on some water and something was wrong with her leg, and she could not get up or walk. I rushed over to get my baby and bring her to the emergency room. Immediately she had an x-ray done on her leg. It was revealed that Aniyah had broken the femur in her right leg due to a growing cyst on the bone. So when I had noticed the limp there was something wrong after all. The cyst ate through her bone and when Aniyah fell, the fall only sped up the process that caused the bone to break sooner than it normally would have. My heart was so broken. My baby was going through so much pain and there was nothing I could do about it. Our only option was surgery. The surgery would be the very next day. I remember praying. I was beyond scared for my baby. She was only 2-years old. Why did this have to happen to her? The surgery went well and Aniyah was placed in a Spica Cast for a few weeks. I would watch her every move. I was so afraid she would hurt herself even more. The Spica Cast was removed a few weeks later and she was fine.

It was now 2011 and I would receive the most devastating news that I never expected to hear. The words "Mommy, I'm pregnant." I was speechless. My daughter Amber was pregnant at 17. I thought, not my Amber. You see Amber was the quiet little church girl. The one that stayed in the church. The one who we relied upon to get prayers through. Amber was going to go to college. I had to accept it though. What other choice did I have? This was my child and my soon-to-be grandbaby. But this was like a punch to my gut and chest.

Jeremiah Javon was born on February 19, 2011. He looked

just like his father. I was so happy that I was there to witness the birth of my first grandson. I loved him as soon as I set my eyes on him.

The following year in July, 2012, Amber would give birth to my second grandson, Jonathon Jacob. I was blessed again to be present for the birth of my third grandchild. Our family was growing at a rapid rate, which was a blessing.

Egypt would be born in October, 2012 as well, my nephew Key Nas's son. I would call him "white boy." He looked just like a Caucasian little boy. His hair was and still is beautiful.

But it was not over for the births because Natasha would give birth to Zakari Darren, who was born on September 16, 2014. He was born on the same day as my son Dashawn. He would have to stay in the NICU for 18 days because he would not eat. He was chunky, and he looked like one of my very own babies, like I gave birth to him instead of her. He finally started to eat. Let's just say he doesn't have that problem anymore!

And WE WOULD BE TESTED YET AGAIN. This time it would be my daughter Natasha. Natasha started having problems with her leg. This started to make me wonder, why were Aniyah and Tasha having problems with their legs? Natasha would have to have surgery soon after Zakari was born. This would be major surgery, so major that there was a halo placed around her leg for months. I had to assist her with the baby and with taking care of herself. She was bedridden. This was so hard on everyone, especially her. She could not care for her baby the way she wanted to. I must say that the baby kept her encouraged. I was so tired from taking care of her, the baby, mommy, and the rest of my children. But God gave me the strength and patience to endure. I had to go through the process. God was slowly strengthening me and I didn't even know it or realize it. Natasha would have the halo removed two days before Amber's wedding. She was determined to be at her sister's wedding.

Chapter 10

It is now 2015. We all were so excited. Amber was getting married to the father of her children. The wedding was very expensive. Amber went all out. I could not believe it. My baby was getting married. Amber got along well with her husband's side of the family. We all got along. My daughter Theresa's father would be walking Amber down the aisle as he was the one who had taken care of her since she was three months old.

The wedding was beautiful. It was in August, 2015. All my children were there, as well as my mom, siblings, nieces, and nephews. The wedding was so packed. We all had the time of our lives.

Life continued on. Mommy's health was up and down. She would be good for a month or two, then just like that she would be back in the hospital or in rehabilitation. But, mommy was a fighter. Not only was mommy a fighter, she was also one heck of a prayer warrior. But still, mommy started to get hostile again.

One time I was washing the dishes and I didn't hear mommy walk up behind me, but thank God my daughter Natasha did. Mommy had a black handle steak knife to the back of my neck. Natasha grabbed her hand and yelled at the same time. I could not believe what had just happened. Mommy had tried to hurt me.

The very next day I remember doing some research about her behavior. What I found out in my research was that mommy was suffering from the early symptoms of dementia. I could not help but feel that this was something so much deeper than dementia.

I brought my concerns to my sisters. Keyonna somewhat agreed with me. But Nisha was flat out in denial in the beginning. It's like she did not want to face what was happening to mommy.

Mommy's behavior started to drastically change. She would go into fits of sudden rage. She would become violent. All of the anger, in the beginning, was only against me. I could not understand it as I was the one taking care of her and she was living with me. I felt that mommy hated me. Every time I would call my sisters they would brush me off. Keyonna was going through her own things at the time which we knew nothing about because she hid it. Nisha would laugh it off like it's no big deal; she will eventually calm down. But, it was not okay.

I reached out to Mommy's doctor on one occasion when I could not calm her down. The doctor told us to bring her to the hospital. I remember when we arrived at the hospital mommy started to push things off the desk when we were checking her in. She was so angry. Her doctor examined her and talked to her, but mommy was not having it. She did not want to hear what anyone was saying.

They immediately put her in a behavioral hospital; in simpler terms, a crazy hospital. They put mommy on medication while she was there to calm her down and ease her anxiety. The medicine calmed her down but it also made her look and sound like a zombie. We did not like that so we told the doctor to stop the order immediately. Mommy came home after a few days.

I remember one day hearing a knock on the door and it was the police. The officer said they received a call that someone being held hostage. I looked at the officer in disbelief. It was 6 am. This had to be some kind of sick joke. As I stepped outside to talk to the officer my eyes widened. There were at least 6 more officers standing there.

So, of course they had to search the house and ask questions. Mommy came out of the room trying to communicate with them that she had made the call. They had a hard time understanding her as she did not fully have her speech back. I explained to the officers the situation and mommy's health and mental state. They understood but they made it clear that if they had to come back again for a false call I would be fined.

I remember being so angry with mommy. I was at my wit's end and I did not know what else to do. So I figured I would call my sisters and we could come up with some kind of plan. Maybe mommy was aggravated with the kids or maybe she needed to get out more. I came up with all kinds of scenarios. My sister Nisha would tell the kids they needed to be a little quieter. But never once did she offer to come take her for a long ride as I suggested. Never once did she offer to have mommy come stay with her if only for a weekend. There was always an excuse as to why she could not. She would say, "I can't take Mommy for a ride because she will have to pee frequently, and mommy can't stay at my house because the bathroom is upstairs. Always an excuse. Keyonna never offered either. I was left to deal with mommy alone. I mean they were there for appointments and hospital stays because they had to be. My sisters held her Power of Attorney and Conservator. I was just the caretaker. I would soon get mommy's bank card, but that made them even more distant because now that Gilly has the bank card she shouldn't complain right? But, they were wrong. I was mentally, spiritually, and physically drained. I felt all alone. But, I figured I had to do this. Not only was she my mother but she was also the one who took care of me throughout my childhood. I felt guilty every time I complained. After all, it was my duty, right?

I started to become resentful. They were going on vacations and trips out of town. I could not do any of those things because I had to take care of Mommy and my children. How dare I even think about a vacation?

Sometimes I had to leave the older girls to care for mommy if I had to go shopping or take one of the younger ones to an appointment. My cellphone would constantly ring. Come get your mama or come get grandma because she is acting crazy again. Never a moment of peace. Mommy and the children took over every second of my life. I had no joy. No peace and time for myself.

Don't get me wrong. I loved my mom and my children and if I had to do it all over again I would. But I would do it differently. I would not let everyone get off so easily the second time around. I cried every day. I would hide in the bathroom which was my only time to find some peace for a few minutes of the day until someone would call my name. Mommy or Gilly or Cantrice.

I was depressed and no one even knew and if they did know they didn't care. I struggled to hold it together. I focused on all my issues instead of focusing on God. I was crying out for help and no one heard me or helped me. Even the children would get frustrated. I would ask them to help me and they would get angry. They didn't want to help with showers and cooking and helping me with mommy's exercise. How could I ask them to help me? This was my mother. How could I ask them to do something that her other daughters wouldn't do? I did not want to put the burden on them. I feel bad even now saying the word burden as mommy was not a burden but she was a handful, to say the least. I would say to myself, why me? Then I would say, why not you? She took care of you through your sickness. Was I doing this out of obligation? That would be revealed to me years later. I spent a lot of time daydreaming then. I just wanted my mommy back. I wanted her to be healed. I wanted her to be a miracle. I wanted my mommy to be a sudden miracle. She didn't deserve all this pain and heartache. Mommy was a good woman. She helped everyone. But at the time she needed someone to be there for her there was no one. I started to even resent myself for being short-tempered with her at times. I was just so tired. I was so tired of her calling me names and hitting and fighting me. I hated mommy having to go to the hospital and I hated her going to rehabilitation, but I loved the peace when she was away. I don't want to seem uncaring or selfish but this is my truth. But, I loved her so much and I couldn't imagine my life without her.

Chapter 11

My sister Keyonna fell on bad times so she came to stay with me. I was happy to have my sister with me. We could bond, something we hadn't done in years. Also, I would have help with mommy. Her older children would not be living with us because my sister had gotten a divorce from her first husband. Keyonna had gotten remarried and had a baby boy named Egypt by the time she moved in with me. We didn't find out about the second marriage until after the honeymoon. We were all upset and surprised. We did not even meet him before she decided to marry this man. To be honest, I was angry. I felt like he took advantage of her vulnerability. Nevertheless, I accepted him because she loved him.

When my sister came to live with me, he came with her. To be honest, I did not like him. I felt like he tried too hard. He thought he knew everything and he had a cockiness about him. He also drank too much and that was something I truly hated. It was during this time that I found out my sister was drinking as well. I blamed him for her drinking, which was not fair to him. Once I got to know him better, I realized he was an okay guy. He was also a really good cook. Things were going pretty well in the beginning.

I continued taking care of mommy. It was getting harder and harder to care for her. Her health was failing more and more. I continued to pray. We continued to have family prayer sessions for mommy. I felt the guilt again. I would ask God if I'd done something that He was not pleased with. Had I not done something that I should be doing? I was hurt, confused, defeated, and tired. I knew I was a good person. I did my very best to treat everyone with love and kindness.

I would go to my best friend's house once a month for a weekend just to get a little peace. But even there I did not get the peace I so craved. The kids or Keyonna would constantly call me. They acted as if they could not take care of mommy without me being there. Which showed that I was really the only one caring for mommy. My friend tried her best to encourage me. But what she did not do was sugarcoat anything. She hated to see me so down. I loved her for opening her home to me whenever I needed a break. She helped me to be strong. I thanked God for her. I truly believe that God puts people in your life for a season and/or for a reason. I believe she was placed in my life for both.

I found myself daydreaming a lot. I felt like God was punishing me. I felt like I would never be happy again. I felt like this can't be my life. At what point did I mess up to deserve so much turmoil and letdowns? My smile was fading away fast. I did not laugh anymore and when I did it was fake. I smiled only for my kids so that they would not worry about me. But, I also felt like they didn't love me. I felt like no one loved me and only tolerated me. I gave so much of myself that I felt depleted. I can remember asking myself if I was to just disappear would anybody even care or would they even notice? Only God knew what was going on in my head. I was never happy. I was angry all the time. I was depressed and no one even knew. Bad thoughts would run through my mind daily. I had so much anxiety about impending doom. I knew something bad was going to happen. I just did not know what it would be or when it would happen. I tried so hard to stay positive. All the doctor's appointments for mommy were wearing me down. All the trips back and forth to the hospitals, rehabs, and talks with therapists and doctors were driving me to a point of almost having a nervous breakdown.

Thank God He held on to me. Thank God for Jesus and His strength, mercy, and grace. If it was not for God holding me up, I don't know where I would have been. I was still praying and hoping for complete healing for mommy. I knew God could do all things. I can remember thinking, if I just kept praying and praying that He would heal her. I always used to think that I was going to wake up one morning and she would be completely healed. He is the chain breaker, mountain mover, and promise keeper, so there was no doubt in my mind that He would work a miracle. I wanted mommy to get that miracle, that testimony for others to see, and be able to say that God did it. I wanted to believe that my prayers made a difference and God would do what I asked because I wasn't a bad person. Mommy wasn't a bad person. We were good people. I begged, cried, fell on my face and knees for this miracle. I just wanted my mommy back. The mommy I had before the stroke.

In 2016, my younger cousin came to stay with me. She told Keyonna a story about her being homeless and almost being raped by her friend's boyfriend. I felt empathy and love for her, after all, she was family. At first, I was hesitant about opening my home to her because of the other family members. She assured me that she had no contact with them and that she disliked them all. I believed her. I used to talk to her and encourage her. I treated her as if she was one of my children.

But then I starting to see little questionable things she would do. She became conniving and wanted to cause division. Mommy kept saying get her out of your house, but I thought mommy was just being her mean old self. It turns out mommy was right. It was eventually revealed to us that she had ulterior motives. She did have contact with those other family members. I truly believed she was sent to my house by them to spy on us. It was also revealed that there was some kind of black magic that she was to place on mommy using certain objects. But it didn't work because God was, and still is, in control and we got her out. I was so angry. I had welcomed her into my home with concern, love, and kindness, and she had mistaken my kindness for weakness.

Chapter 12

God would place four amazing strong women in my life just when I needed strength. God is always on time. First, I want to thank God for Gwen. Gwen is a hairdresser, and she helped me with mommy's care. She gave her time so freely. Whenever I needed her she was there, no questions asked. She even helped me bathe mommy, dress her, and she took over at times when I was just too tired to do it. Gwen did all these things and more and did not ask for a dime. She was also mommy's hairdresser at times. Gwen was the only one who could make mommy smile and laugh so effortlessly. She was kind, patient, gentle, and loving toward mommy. Mommy loved Gwen. Gwen was even one of our character witnesses during one of our many court hearings for mommy. Gwen also had a good listening ear. She went above and beyond to help us.

Next, I want to thank Minister Susan. Susan also had a listening ear. She always did her best to keep me encouraged. She always kept me in the know on important information that I needed to know for mommy. She was the one who would just call out the blue and say, "Get dressed, I'm taking you out." We spent so much time talking, eating and shopping. We were both grandmothers to the same beautiful little girl Ashiya. Susan was so resourceful and knowledgeable. Whenever I was not feeling well she made sure I had everything I needed to feel better, including prayer. That was a praying woman. She always without a doubt went above and beyond the call of duty, not just for me but for everyone. Boy, could she pray. That's just who she was.

I can't forget Sharolyn. This woman was and still is always there for me when I need transportation and when I need to vent. She is so kind and laid back. It's like she does not let the issues of life hold her back or keep her angry. She's given me countless rides to and from grocery stores; to the emergency room with visits for me and my children; countless rides picking up and dropping off my eldest son to and from college. She is much more than just a car ride to me-she is my sister/friend. Thank God for you, Miss Sharolyn.

Last, but certainly not least, I can never forget my bestie, Sylvia. This is the firecracker right here. The one who is going to always let me vent, but as soon as I'm done she is always going to ask that same question. Now, can I say something? She will tell it like it is whether I want to hear it or not. Sylvia is friend I spoke about previously; the one who I would go and stay the weekend with when I felt like I was going to lose my mind. She would welcome me and Jack into her house just to experience a little peace. Along with her husband Jeffrey, we would all play cards into the wee hours of the morning. We would have dinner together and just laugh and talk.

As I said early on, I met Sylvia in 1999 and we worked together at a local motel. She was there with me through five of my children's births. She always spoiled me when I stayed at her home and treated me so kindly. It would be Sylvia who would introduce me to Encouraging Word Church where I am now a member. I thank God for you, Sylvia.

My niece Tiranee would end up going away to college in Washington D.C. Javon soon would follow the following year and attend college in Connecticut.

I remember Mommy always asking where they were when she did not see them. I would tell her "Mommy, they are away in college." She would get so happy and clap her hands. She loved all her grandchildren. She was so proud of them. God was truly blessing us. Dashawn would attend college a year after Javon and he chose to go to school in Massachusetts. It wasn't easy but God made a way with tuition and transportation.

The year was now 2018. Amber would go on to have another baby boy in November of that year. She would name him Eythan Josiah. He was just too handsome. Still is, with the most beautiful hair. So, now I'm a grandmother of 5. Mommy is a grandmother of 16 and great-grandmama of 5.

I began to look for another home. I was on Cherry Ann Street for over 14 years. It was time to go. That was the message given to me on two occasions. But, I also felt the urgent need to move. God will always send you warnings before destruction, and we need to pay attention. Finding a home to fit my family was difficult. But, my God came through again. He blessed me to find a 7-bedroom single-family house with a front and backyard. He even blessed me with a huge front porch where me and mommy could sit and drink our coffee. I was so excited about the move. God told me to take with us only what was necessary as He would provide all that we needed. He did just what He said He would. But sadly, the happiness that I felt would not last.

Chapter 13

The year 2018 was bittersweet for me. A week before we were to move into our new home, mommy suffered another massive stroke. This one was so bad that it took her speech. My mommy could no longer talk. We were devastated. My heart broke. I would not hear her talk again, only groaning and moanings. So, in between packing up and moving, we were back and forth to the hospital. The doctors informed us that mommy would need surgery due to a blood clot found near her brain. I was so scared and unsure of what was going to happen. I had so many sleepless nights before the surgery. I remember on the day of the surgery we were in the family waiting room area and we prayed so hard. I knew God could do a miracle. The question was, would He? Was it His will? I mean, He had done it before. I could not and would not put my trust in man. God always had the final say. So, we waited for the outcome of the surgery, praying that it would be a success.

The surgery took about four hours. The surgery was a success, but the prognosis was not too good. It became a waiting game. We visited her daily and prayed daily. I was so hopeful. I felt like this had to work. She had been through so many setbacks; surely God was going to give us and her a miracle.

I remember the doctor calling us in for a meeting concerning her health. The doctor told us just to let her go. They said her quality of life would be bleak. I didn't want to hear what they were saying. I refused to accept it. The doctor would advise us to let her starve to death. Mommy ended up needing a feeding tube, which we agreed to. We did not want to give up. We were going to take whatever steps necessary to save her. Mommy was in the hospital for a few weeks. At that time we moved to our new home. I prepared mommy's room for when she would get discharged from the hospital.

Mommy ended up going to a nursing home facility for rehab. During this time, I was getting everything in order with the house and the kids' school transportation. I remember Susan being the first guest to see my new home. We sat and talked. We talked about all the possibilities I could do with the house. We had such a lovely afternoon together. Sadly, a month later she would be dead. I remember getting the phone call that she had been rushed to the hospital due to issues with her heart. They were able to revive her on the scene but would lose her at the hospital. I remember sitting on the front porch that night having a cup of coffee when I got the call from my eldest daughter. I stood up and then I collapsed. I remember Jack picking me up and hugging me. I ran to my bedroom and got dressed. I had to get to the hospital. My children blocked me in the room and would not let me go. They said I could not handle it, that I would have an asthma attack, so they would go instead. I was hurting so bad. My heart had broken in a matter of seconds. Not Susan. Please God no was all I could say. This woman was so special to me and so many others. She was loved by many, especially her three children. I could not believe she was gone.

Susan's funeral was huge as she had touched so many lives. She had devoted herself to helping others. She also had a Prison Ministry that she had spent countless years being involved in. She was a special human being and she would so dearly be missed. I cried and wondered who would I call for prayer? Who would I call when I had business questions? She always had the answer and if she didn't she would find the answers.

This was November, 2018. Life went on. Life continued for us all. My boys were still in college and they were doing quite well, thank God. Our visits with mommy were so heartbreaking for me. I hated to see my mommy laying there so frail and helpless. I always would put on a brave face and smile whenever I entered her room. I did not want mommy to feel my sadness. The once healthy, energetic woman that I once knew was gone. It was hard for me because I was used to a woman who always held down two jobs, and took care of her three daughters. Mommy had also helped me take care of my children. Mommy always had good advice and wisdom to give even if it was harsh.

Mommy was turning 62 that year. We decided to celebrate her birthday with her at the nursing home. All my children would attend as well as all my grandchildren. My nephew Egypt and Keyonna would be there as well as Tiranee. But not Nisha or Keyonna's other three children. I was so disappointed with Nisha for not attending. I remember us taking a photo with Mommy and she was looking up toward heaven. That picture still gives me chills. It was as if she saw something that we didn't see. I wanted so badly to hear mommy talk again. She always spoke her mind and would curse me out daily. I used to get so angry when she would start yelling or cursing at me. But now as I stood there looking at her in that wheelchair all I wanted to do was hear the yelling and cursing. I remember my eldest son pulling me aside and saying, "Why didn't you tell me Grandma's health was this bad?" I hid the fact that she was going through so much because I knew they couldn't handle it. The boys never wanted to visit with her because they didn't want to see the pain she was going through. The boys were so devastated when they saw her in the wheelchair and that she couldn't walk or talk.

This is during the time that I would join Encouraging Word Church. My bestie Sylvia had called me and invited me to "Friends and Family Day" at the church. I remember having the most wonderful time. Everyone was friendly and welcoming. And I can't leave out the on time Word from the Pastor. I immediately knew without a shadow of a doubt that I belonged at this church. I was going to make this my church home. I did just that. About a month later, I became a member along with Teonna and Aniyah. Jada, Jayden, and Tamar would eventually become members, as well as Keyonna and Egypt. I thank God that Sylvia introduced me to that church and the Pastor and First Lady. My church family would help me get through one of the most difficult times in my life.

Chapter 14

I will never forget the night of April 4, 2019. This would be the night that would forever change my life. I remember sitting on my couch eating dinner and talking to Tasha, and Tasha's phone rang. I remember hearing my sister Nisha's voice saying 'Where is your Mom?' and Tasha said 'Right here.' My sister then tells her to walk away from me. I didn't pay it any mind. I just figured she wanted to have a private conversation with her.

Not even five minutes later Natasha would say to me "Grandma is not breathing right and we need to get to the hospital." Theresa's father came and picked us up and took us to the hospital, but en route, I can remember Tasha telling him to go to the nursing home and not the hospital. I spoke up and asked, "If she is having problems breathing then why are we going to the nursing home and not the hospital?" I think deep down inside at that very moment I knew mommy was gone, but I quickly brushed it aside.

We finally arrived and I can remember Tasha saying to me, Amber, and Keyonna at the front door that mommy was already gone. I just looked at her and said 'What?" I know I could not have heard her correctly. Amber had a strange look on her face and I could hear her voice saying "What are you talking about?" I remember hitting the floor. I started banging on the door. It seemed like the nurses were taking forever to unlock the doors. I practically ran to the room where my mommy was. I will never forget walking into the room and seeing her lying there lifeless and alone. I ran to her and threw myself over her weeping uncontrollably. I couldn't breathe. Where is my air? Not my mama, I thought to myself. I prayed hard, I cried hard, I asked for forgiveness for me and her. I thought that was enough. Mommy was good to people. Mommy was a good person. Why God why was all I could say. But, I felt guilty for even asking Him why.

On the other hand, I was grateful that we had decided to start paying for funeral arrangements ahead of time. I was thankful that God provided us with the money to do so and we did not have to ask her family for anything, not that they would have helped anyway. Not long after we arrived Theresa and her wife Tabby arrived. We were all in shambles. Theresa was so strong. Amber began praying. When Eboni arrived I can remember her almost collapsing to the floor. The younger children were at home and the boys were away at school. Nisha was not there. She said she was out of town. Nisha was the first person they contacted because she was the oldest and she held the Power of Attorney.

I remember going outside walking around in a circle looking up to the sky crying; my heart was completely broken, still in disbelief. I wanted my big sister so bad. I needed her there with me and Keyonna. I became a baby again at that moment throwing a tantrum. "I want my big sister" was all I could say over and over. I knew she was not coming but in my mind, I kept saying "When is she going to get here? What's taking her so long?"

So me and Keyonna called her as we knew it was time to call our grandmother and tell her the devastating news. I will remember that conversation for the rest of my life. Her exact words to us were "I guess yall did yall best; good luck with the funeral." She then hung up the phone. I hated her at that moment. How could she be so cold? But then again, I should not have been surprised.

We prayed together in the room over mommy. Her body remained warm until we walked out of the room. Everything was a blur to me. I don't even remember walking to the car. I don't even remember who took me home. As we walked into the house, I knew it was time to inform the boys. I also called my best friend to let her know as well. As it was late she assured me that she would be with me the very next day. True to her word she was there the very next day. I had my family but I also needed my friend. The calls to the boys broke my heart even more. They were not home. I could not hug them and give them some of my strength. They were devastated. I thought, Who was there to comfort them at school? But, God had them. I could rest assured in that. Jack did not give me the comfort or the love that I needed. I truly believe that's when the resentment toward him started to creep in. We had lost our dear matriarch to a stroke and congestive heart failure. How would I move on from this? How could we? She was our backbone. This was so hard, but things would get even harder for us.

The next few days would be very difficult for us all. We met with the funeral director and made funeral arrangements, and we spoke with both sides of our family. We gave them all the dates and times as well as the location for the funeral. I wept constantly. It was like I was in a dream that I could not wake up from. Everyone walked around in a daze. We were all full of guilt and regrets. Guilt and regret for not spending enough time with her and not saying I love you enough.

I recall going to pay my rent on April 10 and I received a phone call. I clearly remember the date because of the nature of the phone call. The phone call came from Probate Court. The lady on the other end said to me that I had to be present in court the following day. This was an emergency court proceeding and I had to be present. I then asked the lady on the other end of the phone call what this was about. When she told me the reason, I almost dropped my phone. She said that my mom's family had requested a hearing because they wanted my mom's body after the funeral. I didn't think that I had heard her correctly so I asked her to repeat herself. She said the same thing again. I was livid and I could smell my own blood. I never thought I could feel so much rage and hatred again since "him." I was wrong. I had more rage and hatred toward them at that moment. I immediately called my sisters and my older daughters to tell them about the phone call I had just received. My sisters had both received the same call. The thoughts that we had at that moment could have landed us in jail.

So here we were a day before we were to lay Mommy to rest, sitting in a courtroom in front of a judge. We were supposed to be at the funeral home preparing mommy's body for the funeral. In our absence, we sent Amber and Tiranee. Amber would do her makeup and Tiranee would do her hair. We sat in the courtroom full of rage. We should have been with our mother, but instead we were here looking at these evil people and listening to the lies they were still spewing from their mouths. They told the judge that we did not give them the information for mommy's funeral and that we did not want them there; they lied as they usually did. What

Cantrice N. Costin

the hell did they want with my mom's body? What did they want to do with it? We knew what they wanted to do but it would not happen. Mommy's soul was now with the Lord. So, whatever evil ploy they wanted to do was not going to happen. We went back and forth with these people. We decided to allow them to view the body only. They would not be attending the funeral.

The next day they arrived to see Mommy and they were late. I prayed the night before for strength and patience. I know it was nothing but God that allowed everything to remain under control. He heard my prayers. Every time I would feel myself becoming undone and wanting to lash out, I would walk away from mommy's casket. My sisters and I stood like soldiers in front of her. The look on their faces was of pure hatred and evilness. But the face I would most remember was that of my grandmother. If looks could kill we would have been dead. Now I knew the depth of the hatred that she felt for us. None of them would hug us, none would try to comfort us, and none would utter "I'm sorry for your loss." After they left, the funeral service began. Amber did a beautiful praise dance in honor of mommy. The dance was so intense, yet so gentle and beautiful. Keyonna did our mother's eulogy. The words were so beautiful and heart-wrenching. I was so proud of her. I knew mommy was smiling down from heaven saying "Look at my baby. She made me proud."

I was so happy that my other grandmother was there to support us as well as two of my dad's sisters and my cousin. After the funeral, we all came back to my house and ate dinner. I walked around with my head in a fog. Mommy would never get to see this

99

huge house. Mommy would never sit on the big front porch with me and have our coffee. I had such hopes and plans for us in our new home. I never imagined plans would be made without her. We had Mommy cremated as this was always her request, so we honored it.

After the repast was over and all the guests and friends left we all sat down in the living room rehashing the events of the day. I remember my cousin, my dad's niece, saying, "Why was yall cousin snapping pictures of Aunt Darlene as if the funeral was a photoshoot?" I said, "I don't know. She just better not post my mom's photos on social media." My cousin then said, "Do you think she would do something like that?" We all said in unison, "Yes." We decided to look on her Facebook page to see. My mouth dropped open and I cried as I looked at a picture of my mother lying in the casket on Facebook. We were beyond enraged. My sister Nisha immediately texted her and let her have it. Her response was to laugh and say we murdered our mom. She was truly touched in the head. Such evilness, such cunningness, just like a snake. And snakes are what they were. We immediately contacted Facebook and they removed the photo. That horrible thing she did will stick with me forever.

We all just sat there on the front porch stunned. We talked about what had transpired that day throughout the night. The next day my family from my dad's side went back home to New Jersey. I was sad to see them go. The support and love they had shown us meant the world to me. We said our goodbyes and we hugged. I told them that I loved them and they were off. Little did I know my grandmother would soon be going home to be with the Lord as well.

Chapter 15

The next few months would be a blur to me. I was so depressed and lonely without my mother. I received words of comfort and encouragement, but it was not enough. I wanted my mommy, I needed my mommy. I missed her smell, voice, face, and even her yelling and fussing. I missed mommy's presence. How could she be gone? Didn't she know I loved and needed her? Didn't God know how my heart ached for her? Did anybody know the turmoil, agony, and depression that I was going through? Did anybody care? But how could they know? I hid it very well. I only cried when I was alone. I only cried in the bathroom. I only cried late at night. I did not want them to see my pain. I did not want the children to worry about me. I could not and would not allow them to see that I was broken. I was lost without my mother. The woman that loved me unconditionally was gone. As soon as the kids would go off to school, I would burst into tears. I longed for my mom. I dreamt of her. Why couldn't this just be a bad nightmare that I was going to wake up from, and my mom would be here in the flesh and healthy? But, I was being selfish. I didn't want to think about the pain she had to endure for so many years. All I know is that I wanted her back here with me. I had to keep reminding myself that she was no longer suffering and she was in a much better place. I had to remind myself that it was God's will. But why my mommy? He had already taken my daddy. Now I had no parents. How could I go on? But memories of my mom kept me going. Her words of wisdom had made me a better person and showed me that I couldn't give up. Even in the end when she couldn't speak, I still heard mommy's voice. Unspoken words. Mommy had held on as long as she could. I believe mommy held on only because of us. She needed to make sure we were going to be okay without her. Her death changed me, though. I never knew how much I needed her until she was gone. I started to hate myself. I didn't want to celebrate any holidays. The holidays to me were painful because mommy was gone. I lost my smile, my joy, and my laughter. Who was I to smile and laugh when my mom is no longer here? Who gave me that right? I felt guilty whenever I smiled or laughed. I felt like mommy wouldn't be pleased; that I didn't deserve to be happy anymore.

I found myself daydreaming a lot. Daydreaming about my mother sitting on the porch with me drinking coffee. Mommy had loved coffee. I daydreamed about her exercising on the stairs. I would go to the enclosed cabinet that held her remains and just stare at the Urn. Mommy had always impressed upon us that when the Lord decided to take her she wanted to be cremated. So that's what we did. I had mommy's ashes. I never knew so much despair, grief, mourning or sorrow could take away all happiness. My joy was turned into sorrow, my light was turned into darkness, my smile was turned into a frown, and my peace was turned into chaos. I thought to myself, God your Word says that your strength is made perfect in my weakness; your Word says, joy will come in the morning. So, where is my joy? Will I ever find joy again? Will I ever smile again? This can't be my life. I needed to be strong for my kids and I was. But, who would be strong for me?

I continued to go to church after a brief absence. Little did I know that was just what I needed. Encouraging Word Church lifted my spirits some. My Pastor and the First Lady, the Co-pastors, Ministers, and the members encouraged me. I needed strength. I finally realized that God had brought me to that church in 2018 to prepare me for what was to come. God knew that I would need strength. God knew that I was going to need encouraging words. So He had blessed me to become a member of Encouraging Word Church. Every time I attended service I was blessed with a Word from God. I started to look forward to going to church. My bestie made sure that I had transportation to church. The Deacon picked us up every Sunday and still does to this day. I thank him for that. I also thank his wife for allowing her husband to so unselfishly provide us a way to get to the house of the Lord. I also thank a few other members who also provided a way for us as well.

My days were long and full of sorrow. I didn't talk too much about my pain. I didn't want to burden anyone. The one person who made sure to come and sit with me and let me vent and share my feelings was my daughter's wife. I would get so happy when she would just unexpectedly show up. We would sit outside and talk for hours. Even if she didn't want to hear what I said she still listened. I thanked her for it. I needed it. She made me smile when I thought I couldn't smile anymore. She made me laugh when I thought I couldn't laugh anymore. I finally realized it was God that allowed me to laugh and smile if only for a moment. He used Tabby to do that. Thanks to God and Tabby. I looked forward to her visits and our talks. She encouraged me. I slowly started to change. I didn't realize it until she pointed it out to me.

I spent a lot of time in prayer. In prayer with just me and my Almighty God. I worshiped and prayed to Him. I had to. I know I could not and would not survive without Him. He comforted me and heard my cries. He heard my pleas. My tears were not in vain. I slowly started to smile again. I slowly started to laugh again. I am slowly able to talk about mommy and say her name without crying. God is so good. He wasn't punishing me. He was slowly healing me and building my faith.

I remember waking up on Mother's Day of 2019. This was the first time that I would not be able to celebrate Mother's Day with my mommy. I cried so hard. How would we get through this day that just didn't feel like Mother's Day without a mother? Yes, mommy was and is in my heart, but it was still so hurtful that I did not have her here in the flesh to celebrate her. It was the same way for her birthday. My heart would break more and more. There was a dark cloud of depression over me. Horrible thoughts invaded my mind. Voices telling me that my children would be better off without me. I had to silently fight off these voices. But God. God was there comforting me, as well as mommy. I would feel and smell her. Even to a point where I heard her call my name on two separate occasions. I knew I wasn't crazy. I heard and felt my mommy. I was not afraid, I was overjoyed. That was a gift from God, as He knew I needed that comfort and reassurance. He allowed mommy to reach out to me. God knew I was only hanging on by a thread. This depression and loss turned my hair gray, I lost weight and all sense of purpose. I woke up every morning feeling the same way. Mommy invaded my thoughts all day, every day. I began to pray harder. I needed God to mend and heal this broken heart of mine. I was so ashamed. Ashamed because I was thinking I could have done more to heal her. But, I was not God, so why was I thinking this way? I had to realize that God had to show me that this was His will.

Chapter 16

The ache in my heart began to slowly heal. Oh, I still had my days of crying and sadness, but the days were not as bad and not as frequent. God is greater than any pain, hurt, heartache, and fear that I had. He never let me go. He held me through those dark days. I could not depend on a man, only on God.

Then we received a call from my aunt in New Jersey that grandma was not doing well health wise. My dad's mom, the one who showed us love and compassion. I was in shambles. Not another death, not another loss. It hadn't even been a year since we lost mommy. We packed and went to New Jersey. I remember walking into the room to see my grandma. She was so frail. I immediately thought of mommy. My God, not again. Please God no. The family was there. I felt so uncomfortable. I remember one of my aunts meeting us in the hallway on the way to see grandma and she said to us, "Only family is allowed." My mouth dropped. What did she mean? We were family, right? I mean this was my dad's mom. How could my aunt, my daddy's sister, say this to us? I thought, not again. Not another aunt treating us like shit. I didn't even feel anger, I just felt hurt. The tears welled up in my eyes when I heard those awful words come from her mouth.

I was so happy when my uncle came out into the hall and told us to come in and ignore her, but the damage was done. I will not ever forget those words. I will never look at her the same again. I felt a coldness from my other aunts as well. What had we done or said, was all I kept asking myself. I loved my aunts so much and I thought they loved me. I prayed for my grandma. I thought about all the good times we had had together as a family. I thought about her stern love. I especially thought about the sweet Tabu perfume she always wore when I was a child.

My dear sweet grandma died on January 1, 2020. And the pain and heartache started up again just when I had started to heal. I did not want to attend another funeral. I thought I was being punished. I felt defeated and empty.

The funeral was packed and beautiful. So many family members and friends. You could tell grandma was loved and respected. The church that held grandma's funeral was the same church that held my daddy's and grandpa's funeral. All the memories just flooded my mind. Some good memories and some bad memories. The words that people spoke about grandma were beautiful. I cried so hard. I cried for daddy, grandpa, and especially for my mama. I also cried for Susan. It felt like those that were close to my heart were being taken away from me. I could not wrap my mind around the fact that they were gone. This was unbelievable to me. My grandma left a legacy of a host of children, grandchildren, and great-grandchildren as well as great-great-grandchildren.

After the funeral, we all congregated at my aunt's house. We all just talked and ate. Everyone was feeling the loss of grandma's presence. She had so much wisdom. Even though I was not around grandma due to us moving when we were young, I still felt the sting and loss of not hearing her voice anymore. I felt the pain of not being able to see her whenever we visited. I knew all too well how my aunts and uncles felt. The hurt, pain, the loneliness of a parent's death. I had many talks with my aunt after grandma's death. We could relate and we could encourage one another. We did just that. She was my strength and I was hers.

After all this, I decided to go back to school and get my GED. I was very scared. I was afraid that I would fail. But I had made up my mind that I was gonna give it my all. I could do this. I smiled the biggest smile. After that phone call, I felt as if I had just accomplished something when I made that phone call to enroll myself. My hands were shaking and my heart was beating so fast. To most people, this may seem so small and unimportant, but to me, this was a huge step. The classes started. It is now 2021. I enjoyed the classes even though the math class was very challenging.

I felt so happy until that horrible pandemic hit the world. Covid-19. This pandemic would change the world as we knew it. Here it was again. That pain, loneliness, and fear because of Covid. I feared for my family and friends. I feared for my neighbors. I feared for this entire world. I felt God was trying to get our attention. I remember thinking of one of God's messages in the Bible where He said, "If my people who are called by my name will humble themselves and pray and seek my face and turn from their wicked ways, then I will hear from heaven, forgive them of their sins, and heal their land." This horrible thing would hit the nation like a Tsunami. I would have to start taking classes online. I hated this pandemic. Nothing could stop it though. This virus would kill millions and still is as I write this story.

This horrible virus would hit my family as well. Myself and 8 of my children would catch Covid. Three of my grandchildren would get it as well as my daughter-in-law and my sister. So would my niece. I can truly say we all were afraid. Still, some thought this was all fake. Two of my daughters would end up in the hospital for a few days due to this virus. I can truly thank God that we all came out okay during this time. I can truly say God blessed us and healed every one of us. My GOD, I was so thankful and so grateful. My kids would have to do remote learning just as the rest of the world was doing. I was spending more time watching the news instead of studying and concentrating on school. We had a new President. Most people wanted change. Most people wanted Trump out of the office and we got our wish. I was praying that Biden would be the change that we needed here in the U.S.

The pandemic continued. But slowly the world started to open back up. People fell on hard times. So many deaths and so many job losses. It was not a good time for the world. At this point, I felt that prayer was our only hope and still is. Even the churches were closed down. I remember being so happy when our church opened back up. We needed that fellowship. I needed to be back in God's house. Teonna and Aniyah were dancing on the praise and worship team and they loved it. Something was off in this world. I continued to pray for myself and my family. I also prayed for my friends and neighbors.

Chapter 17

I felt a change in me. I could not understand it. Something was just different. My prayer life became more intense. My fear started to disappear. My worrying started to dissipate. I felt my faith and courage building. I began to replace my worrying with prayer. I began reading the Word more. I began watching more sermons on TV. I started to listen to the words of my Pastor and the Word of God more. My mindset started to change. The way that I started to digest information changed. I prayed that God bless me with wisdom, knowledge, and understanding. I prayed that God would take away any soul ties that were attached to me that were not in His will. Break chains off me. Break any generational curses off of me and my children, as well as my grandchildren, siblings, nieces and nephews.

Jack and I started to argue more and more every day. We did not get along anymore. I saw it coming though. It had been building for the last few years. Jack was not mature. All he wanted to do was hang out and drink. I did not like his ways. He did not like my ways either. We had stopped being intimate for a while at that point. We did not share the same bed anymore. Everything about him bothered me and vice versa. I was quick to point out his faults to him, but I did not like to have my faults pointed out to me. I resented his best friend because I felt like he was the reason for Jack's absence. Then I realized, or God made me realize, that it was not his friend's fault that he would rather be with him than with me. I accepted that fact. It had been right there in my face for years. You let a person do what they want to do and then you will see what they would rather do. He wanted to be with his friend, and he would soon have his wish.

I started to realize I didn't deserve to come second to his friends. I started to resent him. Even the sound of his voice stirred anger in me. I don't know why because he was not doing anything different than what he had been doing for years. I then realized that when I prayed to my Father in Heaven, I had asked Him to break any soul ties in my life. And He did. Thank you, Jesus! I found myself getting stronger every day. But, we could not live like this anymore. The children witnessed our arguments. They were fed up with us arguing as well. A house divided cannot stand. We were as divided as can be. At this point, we were only roommates. He paid his part of the bills and I paid mine. We barely spoke to one another. We did not talk to each other, we yelled at each other. We could not continue to like this. Choices and decisions had to be made.

I remember the night clearly that would push me to make a final decision. It was the night I watched him in my bathroom doing something that I disagreed with. Something broke inside of me. I was sick and tired of being sick and tired. I remember saying to him, "This is another reason you have to leave my house." He looked me straight in the eye and said to me, "That's why I'm trying to get with another woman now." His words did not surprise me, as I had my suspicions anyway. I was glad that he was man enough to finally admit to me what he was doing. What did surprise me was the harsh way in which he said it. He also said it with the children in the next room. I was enraged. I remember pushing him out my door. That's what pushed me. Just like that, he was gone. He was out 15 minutes later. In a blink of an eye, it was finally over between me and him.

Knowing this man for 35 years and being with him for 29 years with 8 children together and it was over. I had to admit it hurt. To be with a person that long and for it to end in the manner in which it did was hurtful. I was used to waking up seeing his face. I was used to hearing him trying to sing the lyrics to a song and always had the wrong words. I was used to hearing him say, "Baby, I'm on my way to work." I was even used to him calling me "mutha-er". I could not believe I was single.

What I was not used to was peace. There was no more arguing with him. He was out of my house. Deep down, I truly believed and still believe this was the best thing for me and him. I mean, I just let go and let God. He wanted to have his cake and eat it too. But no more. I found my strength and my voice. I would no longer settle. I would no longer come second to his drinking, friends, spending all his free time elsewhere, and his partying. I would rather be alone. I had felt alone anyway for many years. I truly felt that he was relieved with my decision to end things with us. He was only here because I was his cushion. I was his backbone. He knew I would always be there to make the decisions, to make sure the kids were taken care of, to make sure the bills were paid. To a certain extent, I was his mother. I say that to say this and I mean no disrespect to his mother, whom he lost as a young teenager-it was like I had to mother him. Making appointments that he would never go to. Making sure he got the necessary things he needed. Reminding him to eat and slow down. All the motherly things I had to do for him. It was like he was another child of mine. It got to the point that when I called his phone his response would be "Hello, mother."

Chapter 18

So we continued to try to co-parent as best we could. He continued to help out financially with the kids when he could. He chose not to come around too often though. Which was okay with me. It was not okay with the children. They felt as though he started to forget about them. I had to remind them that if they had something to say, to address it with him. I tried my best to be civil and be a better adult when he came around. That was very hard for me. I noticed that if I said anything about him that some of the kids didn't like, they would defend him and take his side, which enraged me. To me, it felt like they were betraying me for him. I did not like that at all. My response to them was, where does your loyalty lie? Who was there when you needed to be comforted? Who was there when you needed to go to the hospital, or to doctor's appointments? Who was there to sign you up for school? Who helped you with homework assignments? Who made sure you had food on the table, clothes on your back, and a roof over your head? Who signed all the paperwork for you to go to college and took out all those loans for you to go to college?

I felt unappreciated. I felt unloved. I felt they loved him more. Deep down I knew I should not feel this way, but I did. I mean I could not comprehend how they could defend him over me, the one who was always there. I wasn't a party goer. I was not a drinker. I was not a person who used drugs. I was not a loose person who slept around. I was always home or at work. Every decision I made was always in the best interest of my children. I started to train my mind not to care about him anymore. But I couldn't because that's not the person I am.

I started to notice that me and Dashawn started to argue more. His attitude slowly started to remind me of his father. Not a good comparison. Truth be told, I used to pray that they would not turn out to be like him. I know he started to hate me. I felt it every time he came around to see the kids. He hated the "new" me. He resented my relationship with God. At first, I thought it was my imagination, but soon everything would become so clear to me. God will reveal things to you even if you don't want to see them. Even if it hurts. Sometimes God has to break you and God did just that to me, again. I started to think I was being punished. Why me? Was I this horrible person that deserved my heart to be broken repeatedly? I started to think of all the things that I did wrong. I could think of nothing that bad that I had done to keep going through this pain and heartache. I did not realize at that time that I was going through a process. I asked God to reveal to me what my kid's father was doing. I knew he was doing something. I remember every time I would ask he would always deny things. He would always call me insecure and say that he was only hanging out with the fellas, that I could always come to his friend's house because he was not doing anything wrong. I knew in my heart that he was doing something but I couldn't prove it. That's when I started to ask God to reveal things to me. I just had to be like Thomas from the Bible. Yes, doubting Thomas. I needed to know for sure. When I heard the news, I got just what I asked God for and more. We have to be careful what we ask for. We just may get it.

I remember that afternoon when I received that phone call from my eldest sister. I remember her saying to me, "Are you sitting down? Girl, I gotta tell you something." So I'm like, "What is it?" What my sister would tell me would rock my world and shatter my heart into pieces. My sister told me that my children's father had and was cheating on me-with a prostitute. Not only was she a prostitute but she smoked crack as well. I thought to myself, how the hell could he cheat on me, especially with a crackhead prostitute? I felt anger, betrayal, shame, and hurt all at once. The anger was so intense. I felt like I was going to explode. I wanted to hurt him and her. Then I thought, why hurt her? She was a prostitute. This is what she does. I asked so many questions, but my sister didn't know all the answers, so I said that I would go right to the source. I decided to call my kids father and get the answers that I needed.

I remember that phone call like it was yesterday. I remember it so well because it changed my life. Changed my mindset, changed my view of him, and changed our relationship. I proceeded to tell him the news I had received. He kept denying everything until I kept presenting him with what I had heard. He finally stopped denying it. But guess what? He put the blame all on me. It was my fault that he slept with someone else. It was my fault because I stopped sleeping with him and because I made him leave my house. I could not believe the things he was saying. I could not believe the things he was accusing me of. He did not take any responsibility for his part in anything. He just kept saying, "You kicked me out and stopped sleeping with me." He said he was a man and a man has needs. I couldn't believe what he was saying. I could not even look at him. Every time I looked at him it was a look of disgust. I wanted him to hurt like I was hurting. But he wasn't hurting. That made me even angrier. I wanted him to feel guilty for the way he had hurt me. But, he didn't care. He was cold. I remember him telling me to stop praying for him because my prayers were not sincere. It hurt my soul to hear him say that to me.

So, about a week later we talked about it all. He admitted everything. He admitted he gave her money here and there, which again made me angry because our kids needed so much, and for him to admit to me that he was giving another woman money fueled my anger even more. He truly started to show me who he was. I never imagined that he could be so nasty and cold. I remember mommy telling me this the whole time I was in a relationship with him. I should have listened to my mama. She had seen right through him from the beginning. I remember him even telling me he buys her food from time to time. He was proud of all the things he was telling me. I know in my heart that he loved the way he was hurting me; he loved to see my pain and anger. It excited him. I guess he felt like he was getting back at me for making him leave my house. I was confused at first as to why he was upset at me for making him leave. He wasn't happy here anyway. We both were unhappy with one another. He left the house every chance he got which helped me decide to have him leave. I then figured it out. He did not love me. I was just someone he could count on to always catch him whenever he fell. I had always been his safety net. I finally got it. I finally figured it out. Eight kids and thirty years later this bastard had played me for the last time.

Chapter 19

I cried a lot. I had to get rid of this anger and I had to stop the pity parties. How could I? I gave this man my heart. I bore 8 of his children. This was not easy for me. It was hard for me to let go, but I had to find a way to let him go. I thought I was going to lose my mind. I couldn't go through this pain again. The death of my mother was still raw. The death of a dear friend was still raw. Three heartbreaks in three years. My GOD! WHY? I had to focus on God. I had to keep reminding myself that God's Word said if I kept my mind stayed on Him, He would keep me in perfect peace. I had so much on my mind. I wanted revenge. I then had to remind myself that God said, Vengeance is His.

One particular afternoon Jack came over. I told him to get his lawnmower out of my house. That made him angry so we argued, of course. Then the most hurtful words spewed out his mouth. He told me the other ladies' sex was good. He said these words to me outside for everyone to hear, including his children. He did not care who heard him. I will never forget those horrible things he said to me that day. He told me I had no power. He called me jealous. He told me I was dumb and bitter. It was so bad that our eldest son intervened and threatened him. I can remember later that night talking to God. I told Him that this man had shattered my heart. My first love. The man to whom I gave my virginity. How could he talk to me like this? How could he treat me this way? I asked the Lord to heal my hurt. I asked the Lord to take away my anger. The anger was turning my heart to stone. This was not me. I couldn't recognize myself. I felt myself changing. Changing toward everyone. I wanted everyone to hate him.

The times that he came around to see the kids, which were not often, he seemed to be so happy, like he didn't have a care in the world. My absence from his life was not bothering him at all. I believe he welcomed it. All the kids started to recognize my changes. They did not blame him for anything. I talked about him all the time to everybody, but my talking was all bad. I started to get tired of myself for allowing him to have this type of control over my feelings. I refused to let this continue. I refused to allow him to dictate what type of day I would have. I had to make changes for myself. No more crying. I wanted to know who was going to love him as I did? Who was going to do his paperwork for him? Who would make his appointments for him? But enough. It was time to put my big girl panties on. I tried not to think of him. Then I thought to myself, why am I even concerned about that? He had a woman he was sleeping with on a regular. Let her do it. He was no longer my concern. I can't lie though; I could not wait for him to ask me for help concerning his paperwork. He did just that. I couldn't help myself. I laughed when he asked and it felt so good to tell him to let her figure it out and help him. That made him very angry and I loved every minute of it. I was labeled the bitter, angry, black woman. I denied it to everyone but deep down I was that bitter, angry, black woman. I would never admit that to anyone but God. Only God was the source of my strength at that time. I fasted and prayed. I cried and talked to God a lot. I couldn't talk to anyone about my feelings because they got tired of hearing how I felt. I began to hold in my feelings. Secretly though, I felt like I was dying inside and nobody cared.

I didn't know how I was going to get past this hurt. This was too much for me to handle. Deep down inside, I knew he was no good for me, so why did it hurt so bad to let him go? I knew only God would be able to get me through this, just like He had helped me before. I needed to only trust Him and give Him my worries, hurt, concerns, and anger. I felt the ultimate betrayal. He betrayed me. I could never trust him again. I told him my feelings and it was as if he didn't care at all about how he had hurt me. His attitude changed me at that time. He turned me into a stranger to myself. I didn't recognize myself. I was no longer that sweet woman I had once been. Who did I allow him to turn me into? I even began to dislike myself. I hated that I had allowed him to have this much power over my heart. I cried so much that I began to apologize to God for always crying and feeling sad and angry at the same time. I had to remind myself that God said, Weeping may endure for a night but joy comes in the morning. I began to ask where my morning was. I had to remind myself that God's Word says if I sow in tears, I will reap in joy.

Whenever Jack came into the house and I was watching T.D. Jakes or Jameliah Gooden he would instantly get upset. I can even remember times that I would pray; I always cry when I pray. He would come home and see my eyes swollen from crying and would say, you were crying, but in a negative way. It was as if my crying and worship bothered him. I thought to myself many times that I'm better than this. I will get through this. My God brought me through the death of my father, one of my good friends, and especially the death of my mama. I knew where my source of strength was. But at that time in my life, I just felt weak and alone. I felt this rage. I had felt it before. I never thought that I would feel this rage again. It was the same rage I had the day before my mother's funeral when my aunts and grandmother had me and my sisters sitting in an emergency courtroom proceeding. The very same day we were to be at the funeral home preparing my mother's body for her funeral. This rage was similar; not as intense but very close. I had to keep my mind focused on God. I knew God's Word said if I keep my mind on Him that He would keep me in perfect peace. I had to keep quoting the words of the Bible. I had to pray without ceasing. I had to read the Word. It was the only way I could begin my healing. I asked God for complete healing. Complete healing for every single past and present hurt that I felt. And, I could slowly feel my heart start to harden. That was not good. I knew the Word of God said that one cannot get into Heaven with a stony heart. Somehow, I knew that after all this I would have a powerful testimony. I knew I would be able to help someone else get through the hard times.

Chapter 20

I made up my mind that I was not going to let this break me. I was determined to heal from this heartache. My mindset changed. I was going to show him and everyone how truly strong I was. My mind was telling me that I was strong but my heart was saying something completely different. I remember all the lonely nights. I remember all the nights I cried myself to sleep. I was strong and angry during the day, but at night when I was alone in that bed I would crawl up in a ball and rock and cry out to God. I remember begging God to strengthen me. I had to encourage myself. I couldn't talk to anyone. Who would understand my pain other than God? Who would listen? I had to encourage myself. I thought to myself, why did I have to keep getting hurt? At one point I wanted to just turn my love off. But, I couldn't do that. I felt that if I did that my heart couldn't hurt anymore. No one could see all the pain I was in, they only saw the anger. I only wanted them to see the anger. I remember thinking if I showed them my pain and tears they would call me weak.

How was I going to move on? I did not know how or where to begin. My whole life changed in a blink of an eye, again. I thought I was losing my mind. One minute I was crying, laughing, and then back to crying again. I had to give myself pep talks. I had to make a plan. I had to push forward. I couldn't get stuck, no not again. I had come so far since my mom's passing. I could not allow myself to go into that depression stage again. I remember thinking if I allowed myself to get back in that dark place I might not come back from it. My God, this was breaking me down and no one even knew. I was silently crying out for help and no one saw it. My kids didn't see me, my sisters didn't see me, and my best friend didn't see me. I didn't blame anyone. Everyone was dealing with their issues in life. Who was I to intrude on them and drop my problems on them? No. Me and God had to do this.

All the love that I had given this man. I practically spent my entire life with him. I still could not wrap my mind around the fact that he had hurt me so deeply. But the worst part of it all was that he didn't find fault in himself. He felt he did nothing wrong. He turned everything around on me. The whole situation was my fault according to him. Because I could not take any more of us arguing, because I was not satisfied with just being his roommate and baby mama. I chose me. I asked him to leave and to him, that was the worst betrayal ever. I remember him saying that to me; that I did not care or love him. I remember him saying that I could care less where he would lay his head. He wanted me to feel guilty about the decision I had to make. He always bragged about the number of friends he had. He always bragged about being a "people person" and everyone loved him. I figured then it would not be a problem. He would always be good with or without me, which is what he always stated.

So, I decided to move on. I did not want him to ask me for anything. I wanted him to hurt like I was hurting. Every thought I was having were thoughts of revenge. I wanted that woman's husband to beat his ass. I was hoping that he caught them in the act. Then I wanted God to get him. I remember thinking, I am a good woman and how could he do this to me? The worst part was that he was not even sorry. He did not care about my feelings. All he could say was, it just happened. Nothing just happens. I know he was not walking down the street and his penis just fell into her vagina. He wanted it to happen. I had to accept what happened. Slowly, I began to accept it.

I began to think about all the years we were together. I thought about the good times and I thought about the bad times. I thought, we have 8 children together. Doesn't that mean anything to him? Does he even care for them? Did he care how this would affect them? I wanted them to get closer to me and pull away from him. I realized that it was not fair to them. I cannot put them in my pain, in my hurt and shame. I was so conflicted. I remember saying to myself it will be over soon. The pain and heartache will subside in a while. I remember God's Word, that after I have suffered a while He will restore me, confirm and strengthen me.

Where was Cantrice? I lost myself. I cried and shed so many tears. Again, I had to remind myself of God's Word. My tears are not in vain; my tears will pay off. All things work together for good to them that love the Lord. Yes, prayer and encouraging myself are what got me through. I had to press and move forward. All this pain and anguish must mean something. My pain had to serve a purpose, right? What are the lessons God was trying to teach me? Would I settle or go after what I deserve? I chose me and I was not going to settle. Why should I? I had lost too much already. I deserve someone who will love me unconditionally; someone to spend time with me. Someone who will not only respect me but respect my children. Someone who will not only pray for me but pray with me. I deserve someone I can build with. My life was not over. My life is just starting over. I had to rewrite my life. I had to change the narrative. I had to redraw the blueprint of my life. I had to realize that my destiny is waiting for me.

Chapter 21

So, I took my daughter's class *Vision of Abundance* at Abundant Journey University. This course was intense. She teaches you about the seven dimensions of abundance. She teaches about success and how to achieve it. This course was what I needed at this point in my life. It was amazing. It taught me not only about success but a lot about myself, the fear that I had to overcome, the stagnation that I needed to let go of. The course changed my thought process and how I feel about myself. I love who I am becoming. This confident woman had the keys to be successful. So, I went to classes every Saturday for eight weeks. And I loved it.

I finally had forgiven Jack, somewhat. At least now I could talk to him without yelling and getting upset. I was slowly healing. He moved into a new place with his best friend. I can truly say I was happy for him. He finally did something without me holding his hand. I always knew he had it in him. I had been as much a hindrance to him as he had been to me. This breakup had not been all in vain. At least it taught us that we can make it apart and taught us that we are better off not being together. We slowly became friends. Not expecting anything from one another anymore. He had his life to live and I had mine to live. I was still in disbelief though. I would never have thought our relationship would end up this way. But, I had to face reality. This is now my life. A life without my first love. Just when I was healing, bang! I was hit again with heartache. Not again. This can't be real. God, why?

It was brought to my attention that my daughter needed a break from me and her siblings. Wow, this came from out of nowhere. No warning, no explanation. She just suddenly did not want to be bothered with her family anymore. Even my daughter-in-law dismissed me. And I thought we had a perfect relationship. I guess not. The words she said to me cut like a knife. She no longer wanted a relationship with me. She no longer wanted to talk to me, and she told me that she never wanted to talk to me ever again in this lifetime. My heart was shattered again for the fourth time. How many more times is all I could say to myself. Do I even have a heart left? The only way I knew I had a heart was because I was still breathing. It was only by God's grace and mercy that I was still holding on. My baby girl did not love her mother. This hurt so bad. I was not even completely healed yet from Jack. When was I going to wake up from these horrible nightmares? I wanted to give up at this point. I believed I didn't deserve to be happy. I believed I would never be happy. All these thoughts came back again. Thoughts of me feeling defeated. The feeling of being alone, the feeling that I was being punished for something. I had so many questions for God. I remember thinking I was losing everything. But why? My joy had to come soon. I had experienced storm after storm. My happiness had to be near.

As all this was going on, I was still going to class and masking my hurt and pain. I graduated from the class and the class had taught me so much. The day of graduation was here and we were to wear all white. The ceremony and the people were beautiful. When it was my turn to present my board and read my speech, I was not nervous at all. I remember thinking to myself, now what? What are you going to do now? What was I to do with all the knowledge that I had gained? I thought, where do I go from here? Even though we had learned how to navigate through this next phase of our lives, even though I drew up a timeline, I still was unsure how to move forward.

I needed to get closer to God. I needed Him to put me back together again. I remember asking the Lord, do you see me? I remember asking the Lord, do you see my pain? My daydreaming became so intense. I daydreamed about what was, what is, and what could be. I felt so empty. I remember having to press just to make it to church. I had to remind myself that God was not allowing me to go through these trials on purpose. There were lessons to be learned through these tests and trials. God was not and would not hurt me; He is a God of love. But, I could not see or understand the lessons to be learned. I could not see past my pain and heartache to learn the lessons.

But, I had to learn them. How can I heal if I didn't learn the lesson God was showing me? Lord knows I needed wisdom and clarity. I had to get Jack out of my mind and heart. He was not good for me. We were not good for each other. He tried to tell me he was changing. I started to believe him. But, in the back of my mind, I still heeded God's warning to me not to go back. I remember thinking this is not easy for me, to just let go even though he hurt me in the worst way. I wanted so badly for him to change that I started to think maybe it wasn't God telling me to let him go. Thinking that maybe it was the devil himself not wanting me to be with him and wanting me to be unhappy. But, there was always this nagging feeling that this is God trying to let me know He has something and someone better for me.

I needed to let go and let God. I had to let go of my past if I wanted to move forward. I had to let God handle it in His way and in His timing. I was deeply afraid of being alone. Being alone just like mommy had been for years before her death. But, I couldn't settle just for the sake of saying I had a man. This was the most confusing time of my life. I wanted to run away by myself until I could figure things out. But running away was not an option. My children and grandchildren were too important to me to just up and leave. Reminding myself that I am strong became my motto. I was going to survive this and be an inspiration to someone else that they too can make it. I was going to make it. I was determined to make it.

Chapter 22

So, as time passed I began to conversate with Jack more and more. I remember thinking we can be friends. This wasn't so bad as long as we can keep this friendship thing a friendship and not cross the lines. We talked a lot on the phone but we also argued a lot on the phone. One minute everything was good and then bam! Here comes the arguing. I must admit I started a lot of these arguments with my sarcastic remarks. It was my way of testing him to see if he was changing. He failed every time. I continuously listened to his words and continuously watched his actions. The Jack I knew always reared his ugly head, reminding me that he had not changed. He didn't love me or he just didn't know how to love. I was angry with myself for not seeing the obvious all these years. He was a lover of himself. He only wanted to satisfy himself. He trampled all over my heart. I resented him for it. I felt he had messed up my life and that I had allowed it.

He didn't feel the same way I did. His heart was not the same as mine. He wanted me to believe that my heart was cold. He tried to make me feel as if I had no love in me for him. I started to recognize his tactics. I would not allow him to turn all this on me. He refused to take responsibility for anything.

I started to pay close attention. I started to finally see what Mommy had been talking about as it related to Jack. Why the hell couldn't I see it before now? I did not believe anything he would say. Every time I looked at him I saw him as the liar he is. He tried to get in my head and convince me of all the lies he kept telling me. But, why did I still love this man? He was manipulative. He showed me more each day where his priorities were. His priorities were with his best friend and his best friends' son. His best friends son was supposedly his godson. He treated this little boy better than he treated his own children. I remember asking him, How the hell can you do so much for a child that does not belong to you and nothing for your children? He even tried to be manipulative by saying I was jealous of the little boy and that I didn't like the little boy. That was so untrue. I had no problem with the little boy. He was a child.

He became this sweet person when he wanted something from me. He loved me then. What a damn joke. I used to be his better half. I used to be the love of his life. I used to be everything to him or so he would say. Somewhere in that relationship, we drifted apart, we lost one another. I guess it's true when they say nothing lasts forever. He had so much growing up to do. But, you could not tell him that. Since he was in the streets at a young age he felt he knew everything. The only thing he knew was that street life. He didn't know how to be a father, and he didn't know how to love a woman the way he should. I did not see the person I fell in love with so long ago. Life was a party to him. Life was a game to him; it was a game to him he thought he could keep playing. I could not keep allowing him to worry my soul.

I think it was then, at that point, that I changed. I guarded my heart against him. At this point, he was only my kids father and if I decided I wanted to be intimate with him, then that's all it would be. Sex and sex only no strings attached. I could not and would not ever allow him to hurt me again. So my heart turned cold regarding him. He became a sex toy to me only, nothing more. It was easier for me to see him this way. When I looked at him I would look at him with disgust but yet I still desired him. I didn't understand it. There was this hold he had on me. When I thought about it, the hold used to be love. Now the hold became one of lust. I would say little things to him about me being with other men just to get a reaction out of him. But he still would ask me for sex so that showed me how much he respected and loved me. It also showed me the love that he had for sex.

I started to go to his sister's house and hang out. He was never around when I went over there. My kids thought I was going over there to see him, but I was not. I just felt the need to start getting out of the house more. My kids slowly started to get angry with me and began to question why I was going over there. My sisters began to ask questions as well. I did not owe anyone an explanation. I remember thinking when I didn't leave the house at all they would say to me that all you do is sit home and do nothing. They used to say go somewhere and do something. But they also wanted to dictate where that somewhere should be and what I should be doing. It's like I couldn't do anything that people liked. If I stayed home it was a problem. If I went out it was a problem. I remember thinking they only wanted me to go to church or the grocery store. They also wanted me to be at their beck and call to babysit their children when they wanted to go out or had something to do. They made me feel guilty for wanting to be out of the house. They made

me feel guilty by being surrounded with the company I chose. I
slowly began to feel guilty. I started to miss church services. I was
so confused with the way my life was going. I was so unhappy.

At this point, my daughter was still not speaking to me. I tried
my best not to think about her absence in my life. It was easier
to try not to think about her. It hurt less. The harder I tried not
to think about her, the harder it was to get her out of my mind. I
couldn't help but think that her wife had a lot to do with how she
felt about me now. But at the end of the day, my daughter had her
mind so I could not in all honesty completely blame her wife. I
just had to face the fact that my daughter hated me and has hated
me for a very long time. I would have felt better if she had been
honest with me a long time ago about her feelings toward me. I
remember having the feeling that she didn't like me, and I had
been right all along. But I realized it was more than dislike; it was
hatred. When I finally came to that conclusion it was like a punch
straight to my heart. I remember falling to the floor as the tears
flowed. I remember thinking another love of my life was taken
from me again. My world was slowly falling apart. I couldn't help
but think that running away will ease my mind and my heart.

I still wanted to believe that I would be loved by my daughter
and Jack. But I was losing hope. I was getting weaker and weaker
by the day. I started to dislike myself. I questioned my existence.
When was I going to find my happiness? When was I going to find
the true love I so desperately wanted, needed, and deserved? Will I
have it and more importantly did I deserve it? I was always happy
for someone else's happiness but I wanted my own. I started to

envy other people's relationships. I started to envy other mothers' close relationships with their children. I felt that my kids looked at me as a failure. I felt that they viewed me as being weak. Every time I tried to move forward I always let something or someone stop me from moving forward. Then I asked myself, is it my fear and insecurities holding me back? I had to stop looking for other people and other things to make me happy. If I wanted to be happy I had to find a way to be happy. But, how? I had not one clue.

I had a lot of soul searching to do. I needed to learn how to put myself first. But how could I do that without people thinking that I don't care or love them? I started to think about how I allowed people to handle me. I always tried to make sure everyone was happy. I always tried my best to make sure everyone had what they needed. I thought of everyone but me. I was always pulled in so many different directions by everyone. I never had the time to think of myself or my happiness. I did not know how to be happy. So, all I could do was dream about my happiness. I didn't see a way to get to my happiness. Was it within my reach? Or should I just keep dreaming? Would I even recognize it if and when it presented itself? Or would I sabotage it and have it elude me like everything and everyone else had?

My 48th birthday cake. My girls threw me a surprise get-together for my birthday. I had a good time and I was surprised. They also surprised me with a weekend getaway at a beautiful hotel. I messed up and invited Jack. But, it turned out to be a great weekend. It was a great weekend until we got back and she called (his new girlfriend). She revealed everything to me. All the lies he had told me. Then I'm hurt all over again. I was extremely angry but also a little relieved to finally hear the truth. I could not understand why I was so angry and surprised. He was not my man. But I was hurt. I had to let it and him go.

Chapter 23

So, I made a few unwise and not-so-smart decisions. I decided to start getting out of the house more. I decided I was going to lose weight and I started to lose weight. My mindset slowly started to change, and not for the better. I wanted him to want me even though I knew he was not good for me. I wanted him to forget about this chick. I wanted to do everything I needed to do to make that happen. I remember thinking to myself I know he is no good for me. I know he has nothing to offer me. He cheated, he lied, he couldn't even pay my bills or help me pay my bills. Why did he have such a hold on me? He could not love me the way I needed to be loved; he could not even spend quality time with me. I remember telling myself over and over to let him go. My mind was willing but not my heart. I needed to find a way of letting go.

I prayed to God to help me with my weakness for this man. I guess I was not praying hard enough. God knows your heart so He knew I was not ready to let this man go. I was weak. Only God's strength could help me at this point. I hated myself for still loving him. Every time I cried I would apologize to God for loving that man. I asked God to forgive me for my weaknesses and my pity parties. I was ashamed of myself for my tears. I was ashamed of myself for my fears. I was ashamed of myself for letting God down. But, was I ashamed enough to stop? Was I ashamed enough to stop the reckless behavior and bad choices?

I was confused. I stopped worshiping like I used to do. I started missing church services. I was ashamed of the sins I committed and I did not want to feel like a hypocrite. I didn't want to be exposed in front of the church for my actions. I did not want to miss time with Jack. My mind was just so confused. I didn't know which way to go. After all the hurt, healing, growth, and praying, I was still a little confused. I let my emotions get the best of me and I went with it even though I knew it was wrong. I didn't want to go through this anymore, I just wanted to be happy. I wanted to truly be happy for me and not for someone else.

I started going to his house. We began to be intimate. I remember during the first time I slept with him again all I could do was picture him having sex with her. I tried to erase the thoughts and images out of my mind but to no avail. The images tormented me every time I was intimate with him, even when I wasn't intimate with him. When I would go home, I would daydream and picture scenarios in my mind of him and her being intimate in the same bed I just got out of.

My gosh, what would God think of me and what would my Pastor think of me? Love is a crazy emotional rollercoaster. I remember thinking I don't want to be in love with anyone else ever. Love is not supposed to hurt or be this ball of confusion. I thought, Cantrice, get it together!

I'm better than this. I deserve better than this. But what was better? I did not recognize better because I had never had better. Better was foreign to me. I remember asking myself, can someone ever love me the way I needed to be loved? Was true love possible for me or will it always be a dream that I will never have? I always tried to be the hero and rescuer for everyone else, but where was my hero? I mean deep down inside I knew and know God is my hero, but I also longed for a hero that I can touch. I never want to be out of God's perfect will for me so I battled in my mind. I knew this was just what the enemy was aiming for. I will not and cannot allow him to conquer me. So, I continue to fight every day for my happiness and peace. Sometimes in my head, everything goes silent, but that silence hurts my ears even though I longed for it for so many years. As much as I would like to end my story by saying I was able to let him go, I cannot. I still battle and continue to seek that happiness and inner peace. I have not found it yet. What I can say is I will never give up seeking that happiness and peace. I can say I will never give up on my God. He still loves me, despite me. My story is not over but my story continues. Someday, I will smile again. Not only will I smile again, but I will breathe. Things can and will turn around for me. Time has made me stronger and time will continue to make me stronger every day. I'm doing just fine. My story is far from over, my story continues...